HEAVEN'S Window

BRENT JOHANNSEN

ISBN 978-1-64670-292-3 (Paperback)
ISBN 978-1-64670-293-0 (Hardcover)
ISBN 978-1-64670-294-7 (Digital)

Covenant Books, Inc.
11661 Hwy 707
Murrells Inlet, SC 29576
www.covenantbooks.com

INTRODUCTION

The story you are about to read is true. There is nothing made up and is, to the best of my recollection, a recitation of the facts, events, and plain flat-out miracles that surrounded how my mother came to know Jesus Christ as her Lord and Savior.

The very fact that I am telling this story, in spite of the fact of all the bad choices, poor decisions, blatant mistakes, and flat-out wrong things I have done in my life, proves that God is true to his word and is a forgiving and gracious God. I have no right to tell this story without first explaining a short history of my life and how some of my choices have impacted some of the background of this story, how some of those choices cost me everything I had worked for in my life to obtain that I thought was important, and how even after all the sinful things I have done, did and in some cases continued to do up until recently. That is why I still find it miraculous to me that God forgives me and is still with me each and every day of my life.

Simply put and without exaggeration, short of the commandment not to kill, I have broken each and every one of the ten commandments and have done so many times. To be clear, I, like everyone else that is living now or who has ever lived, has sinned mightily against the God of the universe who sent His son to die for me. My only hope for the future is the faithful knowledge and belief that God has accepted my prayer for forgiveness and repentance.

As you read this story, remember there is only one way to eternal salvation, and there is nothing any of us can do to add to or take away from salvation, only through faith and belief in Jesus Christ as Lord and Messiah can one be saved. There is no other way to heaven except through Jesus Christ. I hope that this true story will help bring you to that realization.

CHAPTER ONE

When it came to the number of daylight hours available each day during the winter, I was never really enamored with the weather in Minnesota. Even though it was only about six o'clock in the afternoon, it was a bitter, cold, and already dark, desolate December night as I left Austin, Minnesota, my hometown, and began heading west on Interstate 90. About four hours later, I was crossing the eastern border of South Dakota near Sioux Falls. If you are unfamiliar with South Dakota, a winter night in South Dakota could become very treacherous very quickly with the combination of icy cold temperatures, the almost-constant winter wind that swept the flat, treeless landscape of eastern South Dakota, creating wind chills well below zero.

The weather conditions, like those I was driving in that night, have a notorious history of suddenly becoming full-blown Arctic-like winter blizzards that would create an absolute "white out" with snow blowing across the road so ferociously that visibility becomes nonexistent. It was weather like I was experiencing that had led to the death of a US Air Force security guard at Ellsworth AFB. The security guard was heading to his barracks across several hundred yards of open field when a storm suddenly arose and the airman became disoriented, wondered in circles until he froze to death in the middle of the field. His body was discovered the next morning. It was the presence of these very same conditions that was making me have some serious thoughts and maybe even a few doubts about whether I had prepared properly for a winter crossing of South Dakota. I also was concerned and worried about what I would do if my car had any sort of mechanical breakdown in winter weather like this.

It was while my mind was engaged in these thoughts and considerations that I realized I had been driving nonstop for nearly four hours. Having driven this far, I also came to the realization that I was rapidly approaching what I had always considered the halfway point of this trip.

Part of recognizing where I was as the half-way point of this trip was realizing that it would be as good a time as any to find a place to pull off the interstate, stop, and get some hot coffee and snacks for the rest of my trip. In addition, stopping would also give me an opportunity to fill the gas tank that would allow me to then make an uninterrupted drive to Rapid City, South Dakota, which was my home and final destination on this trip.

This particular trip was not my first from Rapid City to Austin. I had made the trip from Rapid City to Austin many times in the past. Beginning in 1974, after I had enlisted in the United States Air Force, I was stationed at Ellsworth AFB near Rapid City. I remained stationed at Ellsworth Air Force Base, with an occasional temporary duty assignment, my entire enlistment. I was discharged from the Air Force in 1978.

Whenever I had the opportunity and had leave to use during my tour of duty at Ellsworth, I would make the drive home to see my folks in Austin. After my discharge from the Air Force in 1978, I continued to live in Rapid City. While I was on active duty, I had developed a good personal relationship with the Ellsworth Base commander. When I was discharged, the Ellsworth Base commander had arranged a job for me in Rapid City where I was fortunate enough to continue working with him as he had retired at the same time I was discharged. We actually worked together in the same business.

Based on my past travel experiences back and forth across South Dakota, I roughly calculated that I had about 275 more miles or four hours, more or less, of additional driving time before I reached Rapid City. Of course, my time calculations depended on how fast I drove. As if to confirm my hasty calculations, it was not too long before I began to see the signposts I was looking for that marked the upcoming exit to Mitchell, South Dakota. I had reached the halfway point of this trip. It was one week before Christmas, 1984.

Mitchell, South Dakota, is known as the home of the world's only Corn Palace. The Corn Palace is also Mitchell's big claim to fame. For me, it is the halfway point between Rapid City and my hometown of Austin. I pulled off the interstate and headed to what appeared to be the only open gas station in Mitchell. It took very little effort to imagine that the gas station attendant and I were the only people awake, up and about, on that cold and blustery night. I looked at my watch and saw that it was about 10:00 p.m.

I stopped at the gas pump island closest to the service station door. When I opened the car door, I was completely and convincingly reminded of just exactly how cold it can get on winter nights in South Dakota. The biting wind and cold temperature was doing its best to drive me back into my car. My coat was doing very little to keep the bitterly cold and icy wind from reaching my body.

Pumping gas in those days was nothing like it is today. You did not have to go in and prepay for your gas. You did not have to pay at the pump before your gas was dispensed. I was able to take the pump hose and put it in the tank access, turn the pump on, fill the gas tank, and then head inside to settle up with the cashier. While I was inside, I picked up a few snacks and grabbed a large cup of hot black and, as was typical of gas station coffee then, very strong coffee to keep me awake for the remainder of the trip. I paid the cashier and turned toward the door to leave. As I was leaving to run back to my car and get out of the cold as fast as possible, I wished the cashier a good night to which he responded, "Good night." I opened the door and was blasted by the viciously cold wind blowing in my face as I ran as fast as I could to get back into to my car.

As I started the car, I found myself thinking that I really did hope that the cashier would have a truly good night. As it turned out, the rest of that night, for me, was not all that good. I started the car and headed back onto the interstate. I was not even a little prepared for what was going to happen not long after I got back on the road to Rapid City.

As I resumed my drive, I began to think about all the things my brother Rob had previously told me while I was home. It was also certain events he relayed to me that had led me to making a trip back across the desolate South Dakota landscape to my hometown in the middle of December in the first place. Now, as I was heading back to Rapid City, I began to think about those things and wondered how they were going to impact my life.

As I was pondering the nature and extent of things that Rob's revelations might mean to me, it struck me that, at that point, it had only been a matter of a few short weeks earlier, sometime around Halloween of that same year, that my dad, mom, and Rob were sitting at the kitchen table in my folk's home having dinner. It was during that dinner that all the events leading me to be at the point of my trip that I was now on had begun.

CHAPTER TWO

Now, I don't know what exactly dad, mom, and Rob were having for dinner, and Rob did not provide me with that detailed information. However, if mom was her usual self, she had probably prepared a typical "dinner" of some sort of meat, probably a pot roast, with mashed potatoes (with lots of gravy of course) and some sort of vegetable. There would always be plenty of white bread with butter (no margarine in our house) on the table. My dad and Rob would both be having their favorite tall glass of cool white milk while mom would be having somewhere near her umpteenth cup of black coffee. It never ceased to amaze me how much coffee mom could or would drink in one day.

Suddenly, and without any warning, my dad collapsed face-down into his dinner plate. As Rob later told me, both he and mom assumed or at least thought that Dad had suffered a heart attack. Rob also told me that while they both tried, neither of them were able to rouse or get a response from Dad. Rob said that one of them, he really did not remember which one of them, had managed to call the local ambulance service to come and take Dad to the emergency room at the local hospital.

Now let's be very clear and make no mistake about it. The emergency room in my hometown hospital at that time was not a high-level trauma center. It was a small local hospital staffed by the local physicians who were in private practice. Generally speaking, the hospital had few permanent hospital staff physicians.

It would be somewhat of a stretch to even call it an emergency room. If one were to compare it to any one of today's well-staffed and modern trauma facilities, you would come up sorely lacking. In fact, at one point in the early 1970s, I had worked in the "emergency room" as an orderly. When I worked there, the physicians providing coverage for the emergency room were not trauma specialists. In fact, the staffing continued to be that way up to the day involving this episode with my dad.

Normally, at that time, when Dad, or anyone else, was taken to the emergency room, the emergency room was staffed by either general practitioners or family physicians who would be able to take care of lacerations, provide what would now be called first-responder care for heart attacks, strokes and so forth. On occasion, a local internist or surgeon in town would take turns staffing the emergency room. This was where, and to whom, my dad was heading for evaluation and treatment that night.

Rob had also told me about the care and treatment that Dad had received that night after he had arrived at the emergency room. Rob told me that as soon as Dad was in the emergency room, he was immediately administered care with the standard lab tests, blood work, and a chest x-ray. In addition, the requisite EKG tests were administered, and other diagnostic tests were done in addition to the implementation of additional treatment tools to make the determination of if indeed my dad had suffered a heart attack. Mom and Rob sat alone in the waiting room while all these tests were being administered. It was an anxious time for both Mom and Rob as they had no idea of what was happening to Dad.

Finally, after all the test results were returned, compiled, and analyzed, the doctors were able to make the determination that dad had not suffered a heart attack. Rob said that after the doctors told Mom that Dad had not suffered a heart attack, they also told her that Dad had not suffered a stroke either. There was little, if any, further information that was provided by the emergency room staff to either my brother or Mom at that time.

Rob then provided me even more information when he told me that while all the testing of Dad was going on, our family doctor, Dr. Isele, who was an internal medicine specialist, had arrived at the emergency room. Rob was able to learn that Dr. Isele had been called to the emergency room by the emergency room staff. Rob was also able to learn that Dr. Isele had spoken with the emergency room physician. In addition, he had already reviewed the test results that had been completed. Rob said that after Dr. Isele had done his review of all the test results, he spent a good deal of time talking with both Rob and Mom.

Dr. Isele took time to explain to them that the hospital where Dad had been taken did not have the equipment or capability to make any further or more in-depth tests to determine what had happened to Dad if he were to remain in the hospital in Austin. It was his recommendation to my Mom and brother that Dad be taken to the Mayo Clinic hospitals in Rochester, Minnesota, some thirty-five miles away. Each of the treating professionals and everyone concerned and involved in the decision-making process were all of the same opinion that the transfer of my Dad to Rochester was in his best interest.

As soon as it was possible, the necessary transportation was arranged. Dad was loaded into a transport ambulance; and he was headed, with lights flashing and siren wailing, to St. Mary's Hospital in Rochester. Rob and Mom were following in Rob's car just as fast as they could. After hearing Rob tell me of this part of the story, there is no doubt in my mind that to them the trip to Rochester, no matter how fast Rob drove, must have seemed like it took forever.

Rob had also related to me that when dad arrived at St. Mary's Hospital in Rochester, he immediately underwent the same range of tests that he had been administered when he was in Austin. A new EKG was done, as well as a repeat of all the blood work and body chemistry tests that had been completed in Austin. In addition, expanded testing was done, including such things as a CT scan and so forth which were also administered.

Rob also told me that during this time of additional testing, neither Mom nor he were provided much information or told much of anything about what was going on. They were just kind of left to wait and wonder about Dad's condition. I can imagine very little that would be more stressful for my Mom and brother than not knowing what was going on.

After all the preliminary testing in Rochester was completed and the results reviewed by the doctors there, the diagnosis given by the doctors in Austin was confirmed. It was clear that Dad had not had a heart attack, nor had he suffered a stroke. The upshot of all these findings only meant more testing and diagnostic efforts were going to be expanded to try and discover what had happened to Dad.

In thinking about all this information that Rob had relayed to me, I found myself wanting to stay focused on the fact that this was a man who, as far back as I could remember, had never been sick. I could not even remember an occasion where Dad had ever missed a day of work because he had been sick or otherwise not able to go to work. Now, he had suddenly and seemingly, inexplicably collapsed at the dinner table, and no one could tell my mom or brother what it was that had caused Dad's collapse or what was going on as far as any definitive diagnosis being made.

Eventually someone finally got around to letting my Mom and brother know that Dad would be immediately admitted and hospitalized so that additional and more comprehensive testing could be done. In fact, as Rob told me, this new and expanded testing had already started by the time Mom was told that the additional testing would be needed. Rob told me that over the course of the next two days, this additional testing consisted of multiple CT scans, more X-rays, additional blood work, more EKGs, and who knows what else. After the completion of this barrage and battery of additional testing, the doctors were able to establish a firm and definitive diagnosis.

Finally, after all the tests had been completed and the results compiled and reviewed by the doctors, a meeting was scheduled for Mom and Rob. According to Rob, it was at this meeting that my mom and brother were told that, with all the testing, X-rays, CT scans, and blood work, it was determined that Dad had a cancerous tumor on the upper lobe of his right lung.

Rob told me that the doctors told Mom and him that when this tumor was discovered on the lung, the doctors did not believe the tumor's location was the original source of the cancer. In fact, the doctors told Mom and Rob that the tumor located on the lung had to have come from some other location in Dad's body. The doctors were also confident that this tumor was not the cause of Dad's collapse.

The doctors went on to further explain to Mom and Rob that it was after all the additional testing had been done that the doctors had finally been able to determine that the tumor on Dad's lung, was in fact, a metastatic tumor. The doctors told mom and Rob that this tumor had developed from what was described as a "source" tumor that had been found behind Dad's right eye. This tumor, located in Dad's brain behind his right eye, the doctors suggested was the tumor that was responsible for Dad's collapse.

To make matters even worse, the doctors had also determined that the cancer was a very aggressive form of cancer. Finally and with a hint of terminal ominousness, it was also disclosed to Mom and my brother that the brain tumor was inoperable. There was nothing that could be done to surgically remove the tumor or to slow its growth. All that could be done for my dad was to provide him with palliative care and treatment designed to reduce any amount of pain and suffering that the doctors were quite sure dad would undoubtedly experience as this cancer progressed.

As you may imagine, Rob told me that when he and Mom got this news, they were devastated. When this prognosis was delivered to both my sister and me through a telephone call from Rob, it was devastating news to all of us. After that telephone call from Rob, I again began thinking about how Dad had never been sick and just didn't get sick. This situation was a totally new experience for all of us. We, as a family, had never had to deal with Dad being sick. Now we were faced not only with the fact that Dad was sick but also with the fact that Dad was never going to get better. We also were faced with the questions of what was there for us to do, how much time did dad have left, and how were we to react to this type of ominous, foreboding, and terminal news.

As bad as the discovery of the horrific news impacted all of us, there did appear to be at least a very small bright spot in the middle of all this disastrous and life-changing news. The doctors were of the same opinion that, even with Dad's diagnosis, there was no reason that Dad could not go home and live there for as long as possible.

The doctors did tell Mom and Rob, who also informed both my sister, Sarah, and me in a telephone conversation, that the doctors wanted to make it clear that there would come a time when Dad would no longer be able to stay at home. However, none of the doctors could or would give Mom or Rob any idea of how long or when that time might be after Dad was at home. So after Dad spent several more days in the hospital as the doctors worked to determine and finally stabilize Dad's medications and course of treatment, transportation was arranged, and Dad went home.

To clarify how I received the information about Dad to this point, I was not present at the actual transpiring of these events. I learned of all these happenings and the terrible conclusion that resulted in a single telephone conversation with my mom that followed all of the previous telephone calls from my brother.

In what could best be described as a difficult and highly emotionally charged initial telephone conversation with my mom informing me of Dad's situation, I asked her if she needed me to be there to help with anything. "No, I don't think so," she said. She then added, "I don't know what you could do anyway."

"I can be there for you and help," I offered.

"No, you stay there. And if anything changes, I will let you know," which was basically how things were left until shortly after Thanksgiving of that same year.

On a somewhat brighter note, Dad was brought home, and he was able to spend a somewhat comfortable Thanksgiving holiday at home. He was even able to enjoy a little of the Thanksgiving Day dinner that Mom had made. Rob was there with his family, and Dad was able to spend a little time with his grandchildren. However, and not very long after that, Dad took a turn for the worse. He had become virtually bedridden at home and needed help with all his activities of daily living. During that time, Rob spent a lot of time at the house both helping mom and visiting with Dad to whatever extent he was able.

After the initial conversation with my mom, most of the subsequent updates and information regarding Dad came from telephone conversations with my brother. My sister, Sarah, lived in Germany at this time and had lived there for several years. My sister initially was told of Dad's situation in a telephone conversation with my mom. Occasionally, I had joint telephone updates and conversations regarding Dad and his condition with both my brother and sister.

CHAPTER THREE

It was early December of that same year when dad was rehospitalized at the local hospital in Austin. Once I learned that Dad had been admitted back into the hospital, I decided to return to Austin to see Dad and to spend some more time with him. The decision to make the trip at that time was largely in response to a telephone call I got from Rob.

It was in that telephone call from Rob that he told me that Dad was really very sick, and that was the reason why Dad had been hospitalized again. After my conversation with Rob, I reached the conclusion that I needed to be there with my mom and Rob regardless of what Mom thought or said. In addition, I would be able to spend some more time with my dad. I also wanted to see for myself how Dad was really doing. I believe that the periodic updates from my brother and sister were somehow leaving me a gap in knowing and understanding what Dad's condition really was.

This is not to say that I didn't trust my brother and sister to provide me with accurate information but was merely to satisfy my own need for more direct information. So with no other consideration or planning, I made the decision to leave Rapid City and travel to Austin to spend some time with Dad and to see how he was really doing.

There were only two things I needed to do before I left Rapid City to return to Austin to be with my dad. First and foremost was to make arrangements to be gone from my work and business for an indeterminate amount of time. At that time, I was working for myself in a car detailing business. I had a partner, Rich, who worked with me and whom I thought would have no problem with me taking some time from work under the circumstances.

I discussed what was happening with my dad with Rich; and he told me, as I suspected he would although not quite as enthusiastically as he did, to go ahead and take as much time as I needed to see my dad. Once Rich assured me it was okay for me to take some time from the business as he would keep everything under control, I then turned to make arrangements with my wife to be gone from home, also for some indeterminate period of time.

I, of course, had told my wife about Dad being hospitalized after I received the first call from Rob. When I told her that I now felt like it was necessary for me to go to Austin to see Dad, she told me that she had no problem with me going. Her only concern was whether I was sure that Rich would be all right at the business with me being gone. I assured her that I was comfortable that Rich could handle the work without me. I asked her if she wanted to come along to see Dad. She, of course, wanted to come with me, but she was unable to take time off from her job at the Air Force base. She knew it was important for me to go, and she told me to go ahead without her.

There were a few other related business matters that I probably should have taken care of before I left, but I felt like these matters would wait until I got back home. So I quickly packed a suitcase, hopped into the car the next morning, and headed to Austin. When I arrived in Austin later that afternoon, I stopped at Mom's house to drop off my suitcase. I said a brief hello to Mom and told her I was headed to the hospital to see Dad.

As I entered the front door at the hospital, the very first person I met was my Dad's physician, Dr Isele. I think it was kind of a bittersweet meeting for both of us. Dr. Isele had been Dad's physician and our family physician for a number of years. He had become a friend to my mom and dad and had remained their physician after all of us kids had left home.

In addition, Dr. Isele and I had a very close personal relationship in the past. He was the internal medicine doctor called by the emergency room personnel when Dad first went into the hospital around Halloween. Prior to that time, I had, on many occasions, visited him at his house whenever I was home. When I was attending junior college in Austin after high school graduation, he and I had even played tennis on several occasions.

I had also worked with him while he took his turn as the "emergency room" physician on call during the time I was employed by the hospital while I attended college. Because of this past relationship, when we met that day as I was going to see Dad, Dr. Isele said that he wanted to show me what exactly was going on with my dad. He told me that he did not want to show my mom what he wanted to show me. He asked me to come to his office the next morning. In response to his invitation and with some trepidation, I told him I would be there the next day. With that, we parted company and I went up to see Dad. I wondered about why he did not want to show Mom what he was going to show me but I didn't say anything about it to Dr. Isele.

I went to the doctor's office the next morning as I had promised. I was hopeful of learning the true nature and extent of my dad's illness. When I got to the doctor's office, the doctor invited me into the room where X-rays were reviewed. On the reviewing screen, Dr. Isele had already hung the first X-ray that had been taken of my dad's right lung when he had first arrived at St. Mary's Hospital in Rochester. It actually was quite easy for me to "read" the X-ray hanging on the screen. The X-ray clearly showed a small mass in the upper lobe of my dad's right lung. This mass was about the size of a silver dollar. The very next X-ray that the doctor hung on the screen had been taken on the night when Dad had been rehospitalized right after Thanksgiving.

As I looked at this second X-ray, I was shocked. My dad's complete and entire right lung was involved, and there was nothing to see but the cancer mass in my dad's right lung. The tumor had completely consumed my dad's lung in less than six weeks. I found myself feeling very weak-kneed and was having trouble grasping the enormity of what I was seeing.

It was at this point when I was wondering what could possibly happen next. Dr. Isele took the opportunity to go ahead and tell me, from the perspective of what the X-rays of my dad's head had shown, what the prognosis really was. Dr. Isele told me that his interpretation of my dad's head X-rays and the extent of the damage there that had been verified by the radiologist was that there was one and only one "good" thing out of this entire situation.

This "good" news was that, while the tumor in my dad's brain remained inoperable, the tumor had grown to such a point that the tumor was actually applying pressure to my dad's "pain control center" in his brain. The net result of this "good" news was that Dad was not having and likely would not have any pain associated with his cancers. This was born out by the fact that while everyone expected that Dad would feel a lot of pain, he was having no pain and was not taking any pain medication. I took that as a blessing for him and, in a way, a blessing for all the rest of us. Even so, this news, particularly as to how fast the tumor was growing, still sounded terribly ominous to me.

It was during this visit to Austin to see my dad, and with all the new information regarding dad's condition being disclosed and contemplated, that I was contacted and told that the matters I thought could wait until I returned to Rapid City to care of now all of a sudden needed my immediate attention. It was my banker who called me and said that because of some checks that had been written on the business account and the fact that a large check from our biggest commercial customer had bounced that now the business checking account was overdrawn. The banker told me that it was very important that I needed to return to Rapid City to resolve this situation.

I explained to my banker the situation with my father and asked if it would be okay for me to take a couple of days and then come in to "fix" the problem, or was it something that I needed to take care of right away. The banker told me that, under the circumstances, he was sorry to have to call me but that it was imperative that I come back to Rapid City and deal with and resolve this problem.

Since it appeared that I had no other choice other than to unexpectedly return to Rapid City, I made the decision to leave the next day. Even though I knew that I needed to go to Rapid City, I felt a very deep-seeded urgency to talk with my dad about a very important issue to me. It was also an issue that I felt he needed to hear about. It was like someone was talking to me and impressing on me to be bold and not worry about what I was going to say to my dad but that it was important that I talk to him about this issue.

This important issue arose as a result of the fact that I had recently made a public confession of my faith and belief in Jesus Christ as my Lord and Savior. Now that I had to suddenly return to Rapid City while my dad was in very critical condition, I felt like I was being impressed with the extremely important notion that I needed to share my beliefs with my dad, particularly at this critical point in what remained of his life. I felt that, for some reason, I needed to do this before I left for Rapid City. I also felt it was necessary to find out, if possible, what my dad's beliefs were.

CHAPTER FOUR

Now, as I was getting ready to leave the next day for Rapid City, I continued to contemplate the notion of raising the issue of salvation with my dad. I recalled that my mom and dad had taken our family to church nearly every Sunday. All three of us children had been "baptized" as babies. When we got older, we were instructed on what it meant to be "confirmed" in the church when we were old enough. However, at no point in the process of being instructed in what it meant to be confirmed or in being instructed in our church's philosophical belief structure were we ever exposed to the concept of a personal relationship with Jesus Christ or the notion of salvation because of a personal relationship with Jesus.

While we were basically, as we three kids then thought, forced to attend church as children, we had never been exposed to the idea, or necessity, of accepting Jesus Christ as our personal Savior. I can remember none of the sermons that I was forced to listen to, while attending church with my parents, that ever spoke of the need for salvation. We had never been presented with the need, or taught to consider, making a public confession of any personal belief and/or faith in Jesus Christ as Savior. In other words, our church never taught us how to be "saved" through a personal relationship with and a faith and belief in Jesus Christ as our Savior.

The three of us children had basically been compelled to follow our church's regimen and instruction into and through the program of confirmation. Once we were confirmed, there was no other instruction in the church that I recall or that I was made aware of that we needed or should attend. This religious upbringing, to the best of my recollection, never mentioned, suggested, or taught that one's salvation came through a personal relationship with Jesus Christ. We were, however, taught all the "liturgy and programs" of our church. There was no life, no spark, and no salvation in the church in which we were raised.

What we actually learned in our church was which pew we were expected to sit in and what songs we would be expected to sing as the choir entered the sanctuary. We knew that we were to continue to sing the songs outlined in that week's bulletin until such time as the choir had finished their "processional" down the sanctuary middle aisle. Then there was the offertory where the church and clergy made a large issue of making sure the parishioners were all giving enough money to the church.

We also knew that after listening to what I remember as an uninspired and boring message that we would be expected to stand and sing the weekly "recessional" songs as the choir came down the middle aisle at the end of the service. This process and procedure continued week after week after week until I was old enough to say no more. Once I made that decision, at that point, I pretty much quit going to church.

This "religious" background and upbringing "in the church" and the many years of nonchurch attendance and disbelief in the whole church process that I had lived most of my adult life would never suggest the next course of action I was contemplating. What I was about to do that day, before heading back to Rapid City, would normally have not even been on the radar screen of things that I would ever be expected to do. In fact, what I did that day may even be frowned upon by a lot of people in today's secular society full of disillusioned churchgoers.

However, it was my actions that day prior to heading back to Rapid City that would initially open the proverbial floodgates, which would eventually pretty much drain the lake of any relationship I had, or would have, with my mom for a long time. As if what I was going to do that day wasn't enough, there were certain other negative acts and actions, on my part, over the course of the years that deepened and perpetuated the rift that would start that day between my mom and me, and that would not be resolved for many years.

To be candid, there were many actions I took and other things that I did over the ensuing years that led to the emotional lake being drained even more quickly. These acts on my part would, in the following years, lead to and contributed significantly to the trauma between my mom and me, as well as between me and my brother and sister. I am neither proud of the additional acts and actions that contributed to this situation in my family, nor will I discuss them here. Let me just say that I am and will be eternally grateful for the mercy and grace of a loving God who sacrificed His Son that my sins could be forgiven. But those things are for another day. My mom's story is what brings us here.

What was it that I had initially done that was so hurtful and emotionally damaging to my relationship with my mother, you might ask. What was it that was to cause so much anger between the two of us for so many years? What was so egregious, in and of itself, that, for nearly three decades, my mother and I had little, if any, relationship or contact as mother and son?

The day I made the decision to make the return trip to Rapid City, I decided to go to the hospital to see my dad before I left. I had also decided and convinced myself that before I left the hospital that day, somehow feeling there would never be another chance, I decided that I was going to ask my dad if he had a personal relationship with Jesus Christ as his Lord and Savior.

When I got to Dad's room, my mom was in the room, sitting in the chair that was in one corner of the room which indicated to me that Dad and Mom had been talking; and when their conversation had ended, Dad had just rolled over on his side and was looking out the window. I pulled up the other chair in the room to the side of Dad's bed, between Dad and the window, and sat down.

I sat down and looked at him, and I asked him how he felt. He said that he felt all right "under the circumstances." I told Dad that I needed to ask him a question and that it was very important to me to ask this question. Dad kind of opened his eyes a little more and said, "Okay."

I really don't remember where the courage came from at that time to ask what I felt was a very important question. However, wherever the courage came from, I went ahead and asked, "Dad, do you have a personal relationship with Jesus Christ as your Lord and Savior?" Mom heard me ask this question; and before Dad could make any response, my mom reacted in such a way that I thought she had "blown a gasket."

Literally shouting at me, my mom asked me, "Who do you think you are asking your father that kind of question?" Now, in retrospect, and thinking about it as I write this, I, at that moment, rightly should have said something along the lines of that "I was a sinner forgiven by the grace of God through Jesus Christ," but I didn't. I was stunned at my mom's reaction. She was yelling so loud that I thought the nurses would soon be in the room to see what was wrong.

"We go to church every week," she continued while she continued to yell at me. "I don't ever want you to ask your father anything like that again. Do you hear me?" There was no question that I could hear her as she continued to shout that question at me. I did not say anything, and that comment by Mom was the end of the conversation. I never got a response from Dad.

However, as an aside, within the next few days, I received a telephone call from my sister, asking me the same thing. My sister, who at that time professed to be an avowed atheist, was also very angry at me. She wanted to know the same question that Mom had asked and wondered why I had asked my dad such an "outrageous" question.

The next day, just before I left for Rapid City, I stopped at the hospital and went to Dad's room. I wanted to tell him that I needed to go back to Rapid City for a few days but that I would be back as soon as I possibly make it. He was very weak and appeared to be in bad shape when I went into his room.

My mom was also there. She said absolutely nothing to me, nor did I say anything to her. I believe we were both still stinging from the "argument" she and I had the day before. I went to the side of my dad's bed, took his hand in mine, and had to forcefully hold back the tears.

Dad's hand, that for all of his life and as long as I could remember as having been so incredibly strong, was now weak with very little grip left. Dad opened his eyes and turned to look at me. "I have to go back to Rapid City for a day," I told him.

"Why?" was all he said to me in response.

"I have to take care of some business, but I will be back tomorrow night," I told him.

"Okay," was all he could say.

"You wait for me to get back, okay?" I think I was begging him to wait for me to get back before he died.

"Okay," he said.

"I love you," I told him as I turned to leave.

"I love you," was his weak reply. That was one of the few times in my life that I ever remember my dad telling me that he loved me.

"I will be back tomorrow night," I said to my mom who did not respond in any way other than to give me a look that I am sure was still reflective and full of her dislike for the question I had asked Dad the day before. I left Dad's hospital room that afternoon, went out to the hospital parking lot, got into my car, and headed to Rapid City.

Several hours later, as I pulled into the gas station that cold night in Mitchell, it was that last conversation with my dad that was filling my thoughts while I filled my gas tank. My plan was to get to Rapid City about two o'clock in the morning. I would grab a few hours of sleep, get up, take care of the things I needed to take care of in Rapid City, and head back to Austin to be with my dad. That was the plan, but sometimes plans don't always work out the way you want them too.

Now, as I am back on the way to Rapid City, I am standing beside my car, pumping gas into the tank while trying to keep warm. Even though it only took a few minutes to finish filling my gas tank, it felt longer as the bitter cold temperatures and brisk cold wind made it seem like it was taking forever. Once the tank was full, I quickly headed in to pay the cashier.

Those were the days when there wasn't any pay at the pump stations, and you had to go inside to pay. However, going inside was quite all right with me as it gave me a chance to warm up after standing outside in the cold. By having to go inside, I was also able to get a cup of coffee and a few snacks for the next stretch of the trip.

Mitchell was it. There were no intermediary stops between Mitchell and Rapid City that would be open that late at night. So my next stop, after I left Mitchell, would be several hundred more miles down the road, and that would end up with me being in Rapid City.

As I left the station, I said to the clerk, "Have a good night."

"Yeah, you too," he replied. I can't speak for how the rest of his night went, but the rest of my night went downhill from there.

When I got back into my car and headed back out onto Interstate 90, my only thought was how fast could I drive the next several hundred miles that would take me all the way to Rapid City.

Driving across South Dakota during the daylight hours is monotonous and boring in and of itself. It is this monotony and the stark and barren landscape of most of eastern South Dakota that has over the years caused me to drive across the state only at night. I did this even when I was on active duty and stationed at Ellsworth AFB near Rapid City and was traveling home on leave.

The "night crossing" of South Dakota at any time of the year provides a large block of time filled with plenty of solitude. There is a lot of time for thinking about lots of different things. I had plenty of things to think about on that night. Particularly that night, I was thinking about my dad and how I could get back to him as fast as possible. Getting back to him was not to be.

I had driven what could not have been more than maybe twenty minutes or so down the road. I really hadn't touched my coffee or broken into any of my "snacks" that I had purchased at the gas station when I had gotten gas. I was thinking about my dad and watching the clock, amazed at how slow time was passing. I was also thinking about maybe driving faster than the speed limit so I could get to Rapid City quicker.

As I was thinking of driving faster, I knew that if anyone was on the interstate at this time of the night, it would be the South Dakota Highway Patrol. The South Dakota Highway Patrol were and are not well known for their tolerance of speeding. So as much as I wanted to drive faster, I decided that it would be best, and save me unnecessary time explaining my speeding, if I just obeyed the speed limit signs.

All this thought process had taken only another ten minutes off the clock of the time it would take me to get to Rapid City. As I continued driving that lonely, straight as an arrow, stretch of Interstate 90, now about 30 minutes west of Mitchell, I suddenly became overwhelmed with a strong sense of emotional loss.

Shortly after this feeling of emotional loss had built to a point that I did not understand, I suddenly broke down in an absolute sobbing fit. Tears were rolling uncontrollably down my face. I was crying harder than I had ever cried before or since. I did not pull over to the side of the road even though I was sobbing. I continued to drive down the interstate when suddenly I blurted out, "God, please take care of him." Not knowing what else I could or should do, I looked at the clock in the car. It read 10:30.

I did not stop driving. Instead, I continued sobbing, with tears running down my face, and I continued to cry for at least another half hour or so. Even as I was crying so uncontrollably, I continued driving toward Rapid City. To this day, I really had no memory of anything that may have happened on the rest of that drive to Rapid City. I got into Rapid City just after 2 a.m. and, shortly after that, pulled into the driveway at my house.

My wife was up and sitting at the dining room table when I walked into the house. The very first thing my wife told me was that my mom had called. "What did she say?" I asked.

"She said your dad had passed away," was her response. She continued to tell me, "Your mom said he died about 10:30 tonight." At that moment, I instantly knew where the tears and sobbing had come from. I believe God had let me know in that overwhelmingly emotional time that my dad was gone and that He would be taking care of him now. I could not be 100 percent confident of this, and it would be many years before I was given any other indication of the fact that my dad was with God in heaven.

When I woke up the next morning, it took me a little while before I realized what had happened the night before. It hit me hard when I realized that my dad had died, and it wasn't just a bad dream. What struck me particularly hard was that I was not there with him like I said I would be.

The rest of that morning was a blur as I spent that morning taking care of the what now seem trivial things that I had come back to Rapid City to finish when I left my dad the day before. My motivation in coming back to Rapid City and getting these things taken care of was so that I could get back to my dad in Austin. Now the thought of getting all those things done did not seem quite as urgent as they had the day before. It was, as I was going about finishing all these matters up, I began to think about when dad's funeral would be and what plans would be made for that event.

With those thoughts in my mind, I made a telephone call to my brother. In that conversation with my brother, Rob told me that plans had already been made. I told my brother that I was a little shocked that all the details had been worked out. He told me that a lot of the arrangements had been done before Dad even went back to the hospital. I had not really given any thought to the fact that some of the "pre-arrangements" would have been done earlier. I had to admit to myself that making those plans then made a lot of sense.

Rob told me when and where the services would be held. I told Rob that I would make whatever arrangements I needed to so that I could attend Dad's funeral. Because of the conversation with Rob, I then made the decision to stay in Rapid City a few more days before leaving Rapid City the day before Dad's funeral.

When I returned to Austin those few days later to attend Dad's funeral, it was really obvious that things between my mom and me had not thawed out at all, or perhaps it would be better to say that things had not cooled off. The sense that I had was that since our interaction at the hospital a few days earlier my mom's reaction to me being back in Austin had not changed at all. My reception from Mom was quite cold and quite a number of my other family members were somewhat distant. I honestly felt like an outcast from my family. It appeared, or at least seemed like, Mom had shared with everyone in the family what I had asked Dad before I had left Austin. I really got a strong sense and feeling that I was not even openly welcomed at my dad's funeral service.

I found my dad's funeral to be, at least in some certain ways, somewhat of an elaborate production. I know that Rob had said all the preparations had been made before Dad went back into the hospital; but it still seemed to be a bigger production than I believe Dad, in his own volition, would not really have wanted.

Part of the extravagance I attributed to the fact that my parents had been, and Mom remained, members of the local Masonic lodge. As such, Dad's funeral had a lot of Masonic symbolism involved in the funeral production. The proceedings were also full of all kinds of Masonic displays that truthfully made me somewhat uncomfortable.

However, there were some other things that were very touching and memorable about my Dad's funeral. The one display that was the most touching and moving for me, and not the least bit planned according to my brother, was when my brother's friend, Kelly, an Army Ranger, decided of his own free will that he would stand honor guard for my dad. Kelly stood guard the whole day of my dad's funeral and did so in full dress uniform. It was an honor having Kelly there showing that sort of respect for my dad. And it was a very sobering tribute at the same time.

After the day of Dad's funeral, and really with minor exceptions, for the next twenty-seven years or so, probably to the largest extent as a result of my failures in certain endeavors, personal faults, and flat-out improper decisions on my part, I think my mom and I spoke on the telephone, or in person, less than two dozen times. I believe we only actually saw each other two or three times in those twenty-seven years, and those contacts were quite strained at best. A lot of the choices and decisions I made also affected my relationship with both my brother and sister.

CHAPTER FIVE

After Dad's death and funeral, I returned to Rapid City. In the ensu-ing years after Dad's death and the estrangement from my mom, I had lost the business that I was working in at the time of my dad's illness and death. I knew Mom was worried about what I would be doing to support myself. At least that was what I was able to learn from sporadic and intermittent contact with my brother and sister.

I found work as a full-time armed night security guard for a local security company. I don't think Mom liked me doing that kind of work although, of course, we never really talked about it, and I don't think she thought much of me being so employed. Again, this supposition on my part was derived from telephone calls with my brother and sister.

I continued in the security job for only a matter of months when I was offered a position as the banquet manager of a local his-toric hotel in Rapid City. This job would allow me to use the man-agement and food service skills that I had learned in the Air Force. I worked in that position for quite some time. It was this position that allowed me to participate in the planning and execution of a US Air Force function, celebrating the roll-out and operational readiness of the then brand-new B-1 bomber. It was from this position that I advanced to my next position as I was offered the general manager job of a local hotel that was being converted to a Days Inn motel.

As the general manager of the property, it was my job to try and meet all the guests staying at the property. One of our long-term guests were the members of the local professional Continental Basketball team. It was in this respect that I became acquainted with the gentleman who was part owner of the team, Tom Nissalke. Tom had been the coach of the Cleveland Cavaliers when they won the national basketball championship. Over the time, the Continental Basketball team stayed at the property I was managing, I was fortunate enough to develop a personal relationship with Tom. At one point in time, Tom informed me that he had an ownership interest in a major private social club in Salt Lake City, Utah. After about a year in my capacity as general manager of the Days Inn, Tom offered me a management job in his Salt Lake City club.

I was very excited about this job opportunity. I gave little, if any, consideration to what other people may think or feel about moving to Salt Lake City. I did not give any consideration to other people's concerns or questions about this proposed move. This prideful arrogance also led me to not even discuss this move with my wife. I unilaterally accepted the position in Salt Lake City.

Because I was told that I needed to be in Salt Lake City quickly to start training, I left my home in Rapid City on short notice and with virtually no conversation about this career change. I left my wife in Rapid City and moved to Salt Lake City. I believed that my wife would be joining me once I got settled in at the new job.

Unfortunately, this plan did not work out as my wife was employed in the civil service at Ellsworth AFB near Rapid City. In my selfish motivation, I had given no thought or consideration as to what effect a move to Utah would have on her career aspirations. She made the decision to remain in Rapid City and continue pursuing her career with the civil service. We were divorced shortly after that.

This divorce did not sit well with my mom as no one in the family had ever been divorced, and now I was the first. This divorce should easily be counted as another log on the fire of the continuing breakdown of the relationship with my mom over the course of time, again largely because of decisions and choices made unilaterally by me.

I had only been working for the company in Salt Lake City for a short time. In fact, it was only a matter of a few months when the company underwent an ownership change and a consequent management change. With the new owners came a new management team; and I, along with other managers, were let go. However, I was fortunate enough to find a job as the restaurant manager of the DoubleTree hotel in Salt Lake City. The job at the DoubleTree hotel was interesting, and I again was fortunate to meet several people who were well known in the entertainment and business world. I remained at the Doubletree hotel for several months while I was really contemplating my next move.

Given that I was now divorced and did not know anyone really well in Salt Lake City, I decided that now would be the time to take an opportunity to return to school and finish my undergraduate degree. Upon successful completion of my undergraduate degree, the plan was to attempt to get into law school.

Once again, my mom was fairly upset with the fact that I was apparently "flitting from job to job" as my mom described it, and she probably was right. She also made the comment that, with my "flitting from job to job," what made me think I would finish college and get my degree? Yet still another log on the fire burning up my relationship with my mom.

I had not spent all that long in Salt Lake City when I packed up my few belongings and headed back to South Dakota. I had explored different options for schools to finish my degree, and I chose Black Hills State University in Spearfish, South Dakota. I made this choice after learning that, given the years I had lived in South Dakota, I would be able to obtain resident student tuition status. I applied to Black Hills State, was accepted, and was finally able to finish my undergraduate degree there.

When I first told my mom that I was going to go back to school and finish my degree, she kind of "pooh-poohed" the idea. She told me that she did not think I would ever go back and finish. When I told her that I had already started classes, she informed me that she did not expect me to graduate. When I got my undergraduate degree and told mom that I was applying to law schools, she told me that she doubted whether I would ever get into law school. She then followed up with a great display of confidence when she told me that even if I got into law school, I would never graduate. So the relationship between my mom and me crumbled a little bit more.

Two and one-half years later, my mom and my grandmother, much to my surprise, actually did attend my graduation from law school. I did not like the feeling of revenge that I was experiencing at the time. I felt like I was showing Mom that I could accomplish something she thought I could not. I do not like the feeling I had then, but it was very definitely the way I felt. Because of that feeling of revenge, I had done nothing more than added some more wood to the fire, destroying my relationship with my mom.

Mom and I got more distant after that point, and I did nothing to stop that from happening. It can truly be said that, over the next ten years or so, my mom was very disappointed in some of the things that I had done since my dad's death. I had established a law practice and then made some very bad decisions that led to the end of my law practice. I did some things that my mom would not forgive me of for many years.

That one good thing that happened during this period of time was that I met and got married to a really and truly wonderful woman, my wife, Theresa. When I told my mom that I was going to get married, I believe that my mom was of the opinion that this marriage would not last either. Whether or not that was the case, I do not know for sure. I do know that my mom did not attend our wedding. I have been truly blessed with a wife who, given all my many and egregious faults, has remained married to me for over sixteen years. She has supported me when I did not deserve her support. She has encouraged me when I was down. She urged me to make the effort to write this book and explain what happened in my life in respect to my mom and me. I can never ever show her enough how important she is to me.

Over the course of years, after I started and lost my law practice and continuing after I got married, I would occasionally receive birthday or Christmas cards from my mother. Sometimes at Christmas, we would get a surprise gift of some of my mom's great decorated sugar cookies and/or her really fantastic homemade party mix that she had always made at Christmas time. Other than that, our personal contact was virtually nonexistent. In retrospect, I now lay the blame on me for the lack of effort in maintaining or attempting to maintain a relationship with my mom.

During all those years, deep down inside of me, I don't think I ever really gave up hope that somehow a relationship between my mom and me could be rekindled and improved. Again, given where I was at this point in time, I lay the blame for the failure of the rekindling of our relationship directly on me. I, no doubt, could have done more to try and make that renewed relationship happen. However, I did not take those steps during all of those so many years.

I did continue to pray for her and for my brother and sister as well. I even found time to pray for a change in the condition of my heart regarding all the things I had done that had negatively impacted the relationship with my mom.

The relationship between my mom and me changed very little over those next many years after my dad's death. In fact, the relationship, or lack of a relationship, between me and my mom lasted the better part of the next twenty-seven years. There were very few, if any, telephone calls directly between my mom and me. There were no letters and only one personal contact between us in all those years.

CHAPTER SIX

That single contact came after I had been married for several years. This single contact was when my wife and Mom met for the first and only time at a restaurant in my hometown of Austin. In fact, the only change that really occurred over all those years was a change in the state of my mother's health. Actually, over the nearly three decades that passed by, my mom suffered some very significant negative medical conditions of her own.

Both my mom and dad had been cigarette smokers for as long as I can remember. They smoked a very particular brand of cigarettes that would "reward" your smoking habit with a coupon for every pack of cigarettes that you smoked. As a special bonus, if you bought this very particular brand of cigarettes by the carton of ten packs, which is what Mom and Dad did, you would get an extra five coupons for buying the carton, as well as the coupons that came on each and every pack. The goal was to accumulate as many coupons as you could and then trade the coupons in for gifts and rewards that you could actually select gifts from a catalog that was provided for that very purpose.

My folks were avid enough smokers that they got all sorts of little odds and ends, kitchen equipment, and assorted household knickknacks as their reward for many years of smoking. The total value of these "prizes" was probably less than a few hundred dollars. The cost of these prizes proved to be insurmountable for them both.

I am sure it was just my youthful observation, but it appeared to me that both Mom and Dad were the ultimate fanatics about saving those perceived "valuable" coupons. We even had a special drawer in the kitchen in which we kept not only cigarette coupons but also the Green Stamps and Gold Bond stamps that could also be turned in for gifts when you accumulated enough of them. It would be very easy to argue, although without any scientific proof, that the huge consumption of cigarettes over the course of both of my parent's lives would lead to their ultimate deaths from their respective battles with the insidious nature of their respective cancers.

I am not quite sure or clear when the reality of the specter of cancer first entered my mom's life. I know that it was after my dad's death. I seem to recall that it was in the later 1980s or early 1990s. It was then that I was told that my mom had first been diagnosed with kidney cancer. This diagnosis was made by the physicians and medical personnel in my hometown.

It was not long after this diagnosis was made that Mom made her own decision to begin treating with the doctors at the Mayo Clinic. As I later learned from my brother and sister, Mom had made it very clear that she was going to treat at the Mayo Clinic. She made this decision because as she told Rob and Sarah, "If the best medical care in the world is so close, why would I not go there?" I have no knowledge about what other people thought, but I think anyone would find it difficult to argue with such sound logic. After Mom began treating with the doctors at the Mayo Clinic, I was never told exactly what the course of the treatment plan was for Mom's kidney cancer. I was also never told of any prognosis that may have accompanied that diagnosis.

Eventually there did come a day when I received a telephone call from my sister, Sarah, who lived in Germany. In that telephone conversation, I was informed, after the fact, that Mom had undergone surgery for the attempted removal of the cancer that was involving her kidney. I must admit that I was somewhat upset about the fact that I learned of this serious surgery only after it had occurred.

I expressed to my sister about my feelings and my concern that I had been told about Mom's surgery after the fact. Sarah did manage to tell me that Mom was doing fine. She also told me that she didn't understand why Mom had not made a telephone call to at least tell me what was going on. Sarah then told me that she would make an effort to keep me better informed if anything else happened to Mom. Over the ensuing course of many years, a telephone call from my sister would be the only way I would learn of Mom's medical condition or treatments for a long while.

And thus began a twenty-plus-year journey of medical problems and situations that affected my Mom. All these situations and problems revolved around or were focused on Mom's struggle and battle with cancer. It also began a tradition, if you will, of my sister Sarah informing me of what was happening with my mom and her medical conditions only after the fact.

My sister would make a telephone call to me and, in that call, relay information to me about Mom's medical diagnosis and treatment plans over the course of those many years. During that time, my mom would not and never did call me or share with me any treatment, procedure, or other similar activity that she had or was going to have. Nonetheless, I was grateful that at least my sister kept me informed over all those years.

Sarah managed to do a very good job of keeping me informed as to Mom's medical condition. Of course, the day then came when Sarah told me that Mom's condition had continued to deteriorate to the point of eventually having to have another surgery involving her kidney. Sarah then informed me, again after the fact, that Mom's most recent kidney surgery had actually included the removal of one of Mom's kidneys.

Even after having one of her kidneys removed, and according to the doctors, who told Mom that the removal of the kidney was as a direct result of cancer, my mom would not give up her smoking habit. Sarah told me that both she and my brother, along with the doctors at the Mayo Clinic, continually tried to persuade Mom to give up her smoking habit. All of these efforts were of no avail.

One would think that with the history of Dad's death from cancer and now mom having to have had a kidney removed as a result of cancer that the thought of continuing to smoke would disappear like a puff of her cigarette smoke. No matter how hard my brother and sister tried, Mom would not give up her smoking habit, and she refused to surrender her cigarettes for any reason.

A good number of years went by with no reported additional medical problems for Mom, even though she was living with only one kidney. At least there were no reports to me of any medical issues or concerns other than those I thought I already knew of. Mom pretty much lived her life as she wanted to. She took cruises, went on trips, and most other things a retired person would do.

On several of Mom's trips and cruises, she was accompanied by my sister. As a result of these trips together, my sister and Mom developed a really very close relationship. This close relationship between my sister and my mom continued to develop and deepen over the years. The deepening development of this relationship was facilitated by Mom's continued propensity to wanting to travel and take cruises.

However, the cruising and traveling ran into a little roadblock. It was early in 2001 when Mom suffered her first heart attack. She was hospitalized at the local hospital for a few days and was then sent home to rest and recuperate. I eventually learned that she had also been told to "take it easy" while she was recuperating. I am not sure I ever heard those words applied to my mom. Taking it easy was just not her lifestyle.

During this prescribed and supposed resting and recuperating period, Mom found a way to keep herself occupied by planning her next trip. Little else Mom did during those days could be called resting and recuperating. Mom continued to take care of her house. She was actively doing her laundry and maintaining all the other things that were in her life.

In April 2001, just only a few weeks after suffering her heart attack, she was on another cruise. She felt that going on this particular cruise would really help her in her "resting and recuperating." Not once during this period of rest and recuperation did Mom give much consideration for her continued health concerns.

Most troublesome of all was that she continued her smoking habit even after this heart attack. I guess one could never let it be said that she was not resilient in her recovery efforts, at least in her mind. She remained equally stubborn with her less healthy habits.

Smooth sailing (forgive the pun) was pretty much the standard course of events in Mom's life for the next two years. Then, in 2003, mom suffered her second heart attack. This second attack was a little more debilitating and more impactful than the first heart attack.

Mom's recovery was also a little slower in coming back from this second attack. However, regardless of her doctor's advice and now having suffered a second heart attack, she still would not give up her smoking. Even after this second heart attack, Mom continued in her efforts to keep trying to carry on her life as normally as she perceived it to be and as normally as she could.

Heart attack number 3 hit home in early 2009. At this point, Mom's doctors decided it was necessary for Mom to have stents put in. The plan was to do this as soon as possible after Mom had had some time to recover from this third heart attack. In preparation for this impending surgery necessary for the stent implantation, Mom underwent the normal presurgery routine. This routine included, of course, the normal blood work, EKG, and chest X-rays.

When Mom's presurgery chest X-ray results were read by the radiologist, the perceived "normalcy" of the stent implantations came to an end. The chest X-rays revealed two relatively large masses. One mass was in Mom's lower left lung and the other in her left breast. My mom's life would never be the same after this new medical challenge was revealed to her.

The doctors were able to recommend two different courses of treatment for Mom as a result of these findings. The first proposed treatment option was to remove the tumor in her breast. Mom quickly consented to this procedure and did so with very little argument.

The second treatment option was a little bit more involved and complicated. The doctors proposed that the lung tumor be removed also. The course of action necessary to remove this tumor was to remove a portion of mom's lung nearby to effectively and completely remove the tumor that had been discovered there.

This course of treatment, involving the removal of a portion of her lung, was met with a great less enthusiasm by Mom. As this treatment option was discussed with Mom, she dug in her heels and adamantly indicated that she was not so sure about this procedure or whether she even wanted to undergo the procedure.

Mom asked, and rightly so, for the doctors to explain in detail exactly what the procedure entailed. When she learned that the procedure required a portion of her lung to be removed, she asked,

"How much of the lung has to be removed?" The doctors told her that the portion of her lung that needed to be removed was significant enough that her breathing would be impaired. Her breathing would be impaired to the point that she would have to be on oxygen a portion of time each and every day. That requirement made the final decision for her.

Mom told the physicians that she did not want to be on oxygen for any period of time during the day. She said she saw this need to be on oxygen for any period of time during the day as an interference with her lifestyle. Consequently and making the decision entirely on her own, she decided not to undergo the surgical procedure necessary to remove the tumor and a portion of her lung.

Instead, she decided that she would submit to a chemotherapy regimen specifically designed for her after she decided not to have surgery to remove the tumor. This chemotherapy treatment would be an effort to reduce or stop the tumor from spreading. The chemotherapy treatments were very difficult and quite debilitating for Mom. After each treatment, she would be quite weak, and it would take several days for her to feel like she had any strength again.

Without looking at all the adverse and negative side effects of the chemotherapy, the chemotherapy treatment for Mom was, in a strange way, quite a good thing for her besides the treatment of the cancer. For many years, both my sister and brother had been trying to get Mom to get a cleaning person for her house. Both Rob and Sarah thought that the stress and strain of house cleaning, especially the in-depth cleaning Mom was always known for, was more than she needed to deal with. Now, the chemotherapy treatments made Mom so weak that she was physically unable to clean her house like she normally did. She even made mention of this to Rob.

So in her weakened condition, as a side effect of the chemotherapy, Mom went ahead and hired a cleaning person to come in once a week and clean the house. This person also did the laundry and other similar activities that Mom did not have the energy to do on her own.

I feel it must be mentioned here that even after the discovery of a lung tumor and a tumor in her breast, my mom continued with her smoking habit as soon as she got home from the hospital. It was during the course of Mom's interviews with potential house-cleaning people that, to a person, each and every one of the interviewed candidates commented on how the house smelled so badly of smoke. This became a major point of concern for Mom as she always felt that her home was in immaculate condition for guests at any time. Now it seemed that this was not the case.

It was not too long after basically being told her home smelled bad, Mom realized that in order for her to find someone to come and clean her house, something had to be done with the smell of cigarettes in her home. She then made her decision. Suddenly after being a "multiple pack a day" smoker for over fifty years, she decided to quit smoking. The truly remarkable part of that feat was the Mom quit smoking "cold turkey." To my knowledge, once mom made her decision to quit smoking, she never had another cigarette. Have I mentioned that she was a strong-willed and determined woman when she wanted to be stubborn?

Once again, all of these events that I have related here were disclosed to me well after the fact. Even on those rare occasions when I did have any direct contact with Mom, she seldom, if ever, shared any of these medical or life decisions with me. Only my sister, and occasionally my brother, kept me in the loop as to how Mom was progressing and how she was dealing with her various medical issues and concerns.

CHAPTER SEVEN

It was this history of learning of Mom's condition by secondhand and after the fact information as to why, in early 2011, I was quite shocked at the events that were about to happen. I cannot recall exactly whether it was late January or early February of 2011 when I actually received a personal telephone call directly from my mom.

This was not a call that was initiated either by my brother or sister. I must admit that I was quite surprised when I heard my mom's voice when I answered the phone. And for some reason, I was also a little concerned.

When I answered the phone, I heard a small, weak, and somewhat trembling voice that I barely recognized as my mother's voice. This was not the usual strong and forceful voice I remember coming from my mom. It also seemed like she was having a little trouble talking to me. She was stammering and stuttering as she attempted to tell me why she had called.

Finally, she was able to get out that she had had a recent checkup with her doctors in Rochester. This checkup and the results of the tests that were run at the checkup bore some very disturbing and troublesome results. Mom told me that the doctors, as a result of the tests, had discovered that Mom now had a brain tumor and several brain lesions.

I asked mom what the doctors had told her regarding treatment and prognosis as a result of these new findings. She told me that the doctors had told her that it was absolutely necessary and imperative that she needed to have surgery to remove the tumor from her brain. In addition, and while undergoing the removal of the tumor, she would undergo a procedure known as Gamma Knife therapy for the brain lesions at the same time.

I told Mom that I had no idea what Gamma Knife therapy was. She told me that when the doctors mentioned Gamma Knife therapy to her, she had no idea what is was either. So when she asked the doctors what Gamma Knife therapy was, she was told that it is a treatment that would narrowly target only the lesions in her brain and would eliminate any need for more widespread radiation therapy. Mom was told that while the Gamma Knife therapy was being conducted, the brain tumor would actually be removed from her brain at the same time.

Also in this telephone conversation, Mom spent a few minutes describing in great detail this course of treatment for me. She also described her apparently urgent need for surgery and some form of chemotherapy. She then stunned me with a request that was not really expected, and I was not really sure I heard her properly.

Mom spent several more minutes explaining in great detail and telling me again about her planned procedures and treatment. After her discussion regarding the planned procedures and treatment, she ventured into an area of discussion that I was really not ready for, nor did I expect at all. Mom told me that she wanted me there. "You what?" I said in response. Mom then told me again that she would like me to be there while she was undergoing this surgery and Gamma Knife therapy. She said she would like me there if there was any way that I could make it.

Now it is not like I would not make every effort to be there, but Mom made this request of me on the very day before her surgery was scheduled. Not a lot of notice, but there it was.

"Of course, I will be there," I told her. I did not tell her that I was actually more than a little surprised and a little stunned that she had called me at all and was asking me to be there. Not one time before had Mom ever asked me to be at any of her other treatments or surgeries. I found myself somewhat at a loss as to how to take this request.

When Mom made this telephone call to me, my wife, Theresa, and I were living in Oklahoma. I assured Mom that I would be there as quickly as possible. I told her that I would leave immediately and that I would be there before she went into surgery the next day.

Mom took that opportunity to tell me that she did not want me to rush; and that since she would be taken into surgery very early in the morning, she thought it would be better if I were there when she came out of surgery.

I dropped everything that I was doing, told Theresa that I was heading to Minnesota to be with Mom. Theresa knew of the years in which there was a lack of any meaningful relationship between me and my mom. There was no hesitation on Theresa's end of things. She told me to go and spend as much time as I needed.

I left almost at once and made the normally nearly nine-hour trip in somewhat less time than that. I was able to get home, get checked into a hotel room to spend the rest of the night at the hotel before Mom's surgery. This way, I could head to the hospital early in the morning. I would be there for Mom when she came out of the recovery room just as she had asked me to be.

When I arrived at the hospital that morning and of no surprise to me, my brother was already there. Rob told me that Mom had already been taken for surgery and that it would be a couple of hours before she would be out of surgery and in a recovery room. Although nothing was ever said, I kind of believe that Rob was a little upset that I had not been there before Mom went into surgery. But since he did not say anything, I did not feel it necessary to bring up the subject either.

Rob and I spent the entire waiting time in the family waiting room. There was no conversation between us, and neither of us seemed to be too interested in talking anyway. I believe this was especially so because it seemed that we were both alone in our thoughts about what was going on with Mom. Rob looked to me like he was on the verge of tears. I think maybe he was having a few flashback memories of what Dad had gone through with his cancer.

After what could not have been more than a couple of hours, although waiting made it seem much longer, a nurse came out and told Rob and I that the surgery was over and that mom was in the recovery room. Shortly after that and while waiting to go in to see Mom in the recovery room, we met with her surgeon. The doctor explained to us that everything had gone well.

He said that the Gamma Knife therapy had gone exceptionally well. He told us that when it came time to remove the tumor from Mom's brain, the tumor had virtually "popped' out of her brain when they attempted to remove it. The doctor went on to tell us that the Gamma Knife therapy treatment should give Mom a "significant period" of relief from any more brain lesions. Of course, when we asked the doctor, he could not define what a "significant period" of time was.

The doctor then took a few minutes to explain the course of treatment that was anticipated for Mom over the next several weeks. Rob and I were told that once mom had recovered from her surgery, a course of chemotherapy would be absolutely necessary to deal with any lesions that may not have shown up on the brain scan. He then indicated to us that this chemotherapy treatment could "wait until she is feeling better and well recovered." All in all, the report we got seemed to be fairly positive at least under the circumstances. The doctor then asked us if we had any more questions. We told him we did not have any more questions, at least for now. He told us the floor nurse would be out shortly just as soon as Mom was ready for visitors.

Rob and I did not have much longer to wait. In what could have been no more than a few minutes, the floor nurse came into the hallway and called us. The nurse told us that Mom had been returned to her room. She also told us that we were more than welcome to visit with Mom but only for just a little while.

When we entered Mom's room, it was quite obvious that she was very weak and really not able to do much talking or anything else. Her head was wrapped in a postsurgical dressing. There were several IV lines delivering whatever medications she was receiving. She was, as expected, quite groggy as well.

Both Rob and I spent the next several minutes trying to talk with and to Mom. She was really very groggy and slow in responding to anything we said or asked her. All the while we were there, the nurse was in and out of the room. She was doing a great job of constantly checking to make sure Mom was comfortable and feeling okay.

It was not too long after we began our efforts to try and talk with Mom that she suddenly said she was tired and that she thought it was best that Rob and I should probably be heading back to Austin so she could get some rest. So after both Rob and I gave Mom a kiss on her forehead, we left Mom's room, got into our cars, and headed back to Austin.

The entire time I was driving back to Austin, I was thinking about staying at Mom's house instead of the hotel. I am not sure why I thought that I should do that but finally made the decision to stay at Mom's instead of returning to the hotel. As I continued to think about the situation, I had decided I was going to stay as long as I needed too, I thought it would be better for me to be at her house if she needed me. And after all, if I did otherwise, Mom would be coming home to an empty house.

There were some other thoughts that occupied my mind on that drive back to Austin. I thought about the fact that I continued to be quite surprised that I had even gotten a call from my Mom just two days before, asking me to be there with her. I do have to admit that, deep inside of me, I was very glad I had gotten that telephone call. I think that I really believed that this was perhaps the last and only chance we would have to make any kind of effort at restoring our relationship.

Once I made the decision to stay that second night at Mom's house, I stayed there for the rest of the time I was in town. I continued to live at Mom's house and drove to Rochester every day to see Mom and spend as much time with her as I could while she was still in the hospital.

Under the circumstances, I wanted to make sure she was doing okay well before I made any plans to return to my home. Again, I am so grateful to my wife during this time. Not once did she question my staying in Minnesota with my mom. In fact, the only questions she asked me were in relationship to how mom was doing after her surgery.

Several more days passed before Mom was finally released from the hospital. She was sent home to continue her recovery and recuperation. When she got home, she wasted no time and headed right to bed. She said she was "really tired" and fell asleep almost immediately. I did not doubt how tired she said she was seeing as how weak she appeared.

It took another few days of never leaving the bed except to use the bathroom before Mom said she was feeling okay. She was able to get out of bed relatively easily, take herself to the bathroom, get herself something to eat, and make herself some coffee.

She told me that she felt good enough that I should probably head back home and get back to my wife. "I don't want Theresa to think I kidnapped you," she jokingly said. So with Mom's blessing and assurance that she was okay, the next day, I loaded up my car, filled the gas tank, and headed back to my home in Oklahoma.

A couple of weeks after I got home, I received another surprise call directly from my mom. She had called to tell me that her chemotherapy had started and ended after only couple of days. Her treatment had started as soon as Mom had told the doctors she felt that she could handle the treatments. However, because of Mom's severe adverse reaction to the drugs used for her chemotherapy treatment, the treatment was stopped after only a few days after it had been started. Mom would never undergo any more chemotherapy treatment of any kind for her cancer.

Chapter Eight

Once I had returned to Oklahoma, I began to make it a practice to call my mom quite regularly. I wanted to check on her, see how she was feeling, and to check on how she was getting along in general. I guess I was hoping that she would realize that I cared about her and how she was doing. I think now that this was also for my benefit as well. In our conversations, she would tell me most days that she was feeling fine, but then again there would be some days that were not so good.

Mom told me that she really was pretty limited in her mobility. She blamed this on a number of different factors. First, she said it was her surgery that had really impacted her ability to move around. Secondly, it was not only her surgery but also some cumulative effect of her short-term chemotherapy treatment. Finally, and with some hesitancy to admit it, she blamed the continued effects of her cancer.

She said she spent most of her time in her bedroom with her telephone, TV remote, and her cat to keep her company. She was able to get out of her bed, get herself into her wheelchair to go to the bathroom and to the kitchen to get herself something to eat. Of course, when I asked her if there was anything I could do, she continually told me no; and if there was anything that I could do, she would be sure to let me know.

Mom remained very independent in her mind and didn't like to and didn't want to ask anyone for help with anything. She did sometimes need my brother to come over and help her with a few things around the house. Most of the time, the things he did were little home repair and maintenance-type issues, but occasionally there were some big things he had to do. Most strikingly was when he had to fill sandbags to keep the backyard and maybe the house from flooding when a nearby creek flooded.

Most evenings, Rob would go over to Mom's house after he was done working and make dinner for her. Oftentimes he would have his dinner with Mom and spend some time with her after they ate.

Other than my telephone calls, which I tried to make as often as I could, I really did not hear much from Mom until May 11, 2011. That afternoon, I got another telephone call from my Mom. She did not sound very good; and in fact, she actually sounded quite depressed. I asked her what was wrong.

Once again, Mom seemed to be having trouble and was struggling to talk and relay information to me. She told me that at her most recent doctor appointment, which had actually occurred earlier that day, the doctors had discovered more brain lesions. Mom now needed to go back to the hospital for another Gamma Knife therapy treatment. That was not all. In addition to the Gamma Knife treatment, she also was going to be subjected to a course of full brain radiation treatment. She was told that the brain radiation treatment would be done on an outpatient basis after the Gamma Knife treatment. She then informed me that the doctors had told her the brain radiation treatment was fifteen consecutive days of treatment.

This information was devastating news to Mom. I believe the reason this news was especially devastating to Mom was of her perception of the "success" of the previous Gamma Knife treatment. She thought that she had beaten her brain cancer and was actually on the road to some form of recovery. This newest piece of news absolutely knocked her for a loop. This suspicion of mine was confirmed when Mom made yet again an unusual and totally unexpected request of me.

The request that Mom eventually made of me was as unexpected then as any other request she had made of me up to that point. Over the course of Mom's entire illness, she had relied almost exclusively on my brother as her on-call provider. When called or needed, Rob would drop whatever he was doing to take care of Mom's needs whatever they may be. He was reliable, loyal, and was always there whenever Mom needed him. He sacrificed so much to provide for Mom that I know that Sarah and I can never repay him for all that he did for Mom. For her now to call me immediately raised questions in my mind of what it could possibly be that she wanted from me. I also wondered what exactly was going on with her.

I found myself quite surprised again at this information. I also was not quite sure of how I should take this information. In addition, and even more important was that I was also wondering how mom had really taken this new and negative information. I asked mom if she had been told, whether or not this would be the extent of her treatment or could she expect more and other types of treatment as well. She told me that she was not sure if this was the totality of the treatment she would need or not.

There was a lull in our conversation at that point. When Mom began speaking again, she hit me with up to this point another unexpected request. Mom took a deep breath, and she then asked me if I could come back to Austin and be the one who would take her back and forth for her daily radiation treatments. She told me that she really didn't need me for the entire fifteen days but only for the last week or so of treatment. She explained to me that she did not need me for all the fifteen days because as she said, "I have other friends who could take me to my appointments for the first part of the treatments.

This request was again totally and completely unexpected. I told mom that she needed to "let me make sure there is nothing keeping me here that I need to do first. I will call you back in just a little bit." Of course, there were arrangements that would have to be made to accommodate the time that Mom needed me to run her to and from her appointments. However, in light of the fact, Mom and I really had no relationship for all those many years; and given I was actually trying to find some way to re-establish a relationship with her, there was no way I was going to turn her down.

So dealing with all the necessary scheduling arrangements and the fact that Theresa continued to be supportive of my efforts to re-establish a relationship with my mom, I actually looked forward to being able to help my mom out with her request. I called Mom back and told her that I would definitely be there to help with the transportation chores. It was then that she hit me with yet another surprise request.

All throughout this entire telephone conversation, I noticed that Mom again sounded very tired and naturally a little depressed. Finally, after another seemingly long pause, Mom asked me specifically if there was any way I could be home on Wednesday, May 25. When I asked why that specific date, Mom told me that was the day she was scheduled to have her second Gamma Knife treatment. I immediately got the sense that this was a very deeply thought-out and important request my mom was making.

Given my feeling of how important this request was for Mom, I assured her that I would be there Wednesday before she went in for her treatment. Once again, she informed me that I did not need to be at the hospital first thing in the morning as she would be going in for her treatment very early in the morning and that she would be returning home that afternoon. She just wanted to be sure that I would be there when she got home.

I arrived in Austin, Wednesday, May 25, just as Mom had requested. It was around 4:00 p.m. when I actually drove into town. I called Mom as I entered town to let her know that I had arrived safely and so she would know where I was. As it turned out, she had just gotten home herself. I told her I was in town and that I would be right over to see her. She told me that I didn't need to come right over as she was "pretty tired" and was just going to go to bed and rest. Of course, I did not have any objection to that. So as far as I know, Mom went right to bed that Wednesday afternoon, and I again went to check into a hotel.

That evening, while I was sitting in my hotel room, I spent most of the time thinking. In fact, I spent a lot of the time thinking about what was happening with my mom. I wondered what she was thinking about the situation. I wondered if she was thinking along the same lines as I was. With this new situation and the prognosis she had received, could anyone but wonder how much time was really left for her. I was wondering if she was going to have any meaningful recovery from this new round of procedures and the subsequent chemotherapy treatments.

However, at that point, what felt most important to me at the time in my thought process was how could I talk to my mom about her salvation. I was worried if I tried to talk with her about this subject, she would get upset and start yelling at me like she did when I asked my dad the same type of questions. As I continued to reflect on this question, it came to me that this was most likely the real reason I had ended up in Austin again. I then felt and believed that somehow the opportunity for this discussion would present itself in some way.

I did not sleep especially well that Wednesday after I checked into the hotel. There were many divergent thoughts going through my mind that night. They were those close, private thoughts that centered around my own salvation—how I had been acting and the things that I had done over the years created a real doubt as to whether I had really accepted Jesus Christ as my Savior or not, thoughts of how, after all the years and distance that had grown between Mom and I, largely as a result of my actions, could I present the issue and importance of salvation to my mom. I was clearly laboring under the false pretense that Mom's salvation was up to me and that I had to "persuade" her to be saved. I also had thoughts about what would I do and how would I act if Mom got mad at me like she did in Dad's hospital room.

Eventually and quite late, I managed to fall asleep Wednesday night. When I woke up Thursday morning, I had no more thoughts about how I was going to approach Mom with what I really needed to share with her. What I did know for certain was that I desperately needed a cup of coffee before I headed over to Mom's house. Fortunately for me, there was a nice little coffee shop right across the street from my hotel. I made that coffee shop my first stop after taking a shower and getting dressed. I ran into the coffee shop, got my fresh cup of coffee, and jumped back in the car. I headed over to Mom's house to see how she was doing that morning.

CHAPTER NINE

When I got to Mom's house, I thought about just going in the door like we used to do as kids. I considered the situation was somewhat different now, so I knocked on the door. There was no answer to my knock, so I checked to see if the door was open. The door in fact was open, so I went ahead and let myself in. I expected to find Mom either sitting at the kitchen table with a cup of coffee in her hand or in the living room watching television. However, she was not in the kitchen or in the living room.

Instead, I found her still in her bed, awake and watching television in her room. I must admit that I was somewhat surprised at what I saw in Mom's room. She was lying in bed with all of her blankets pulled up almost to her chin. She looked so very much different from the last time I had seen her. While it had not been that long from the last time I had seen my mother, she had now lost a lot of weight and looked remarkably haggard, more haggard and much thinner than I had ever seen her.

"How are you feeling?" were the first words out of my mouth.

She told me that she "felt fine, maybe just a little tired."

"Can I get you anything?" I asked.

Seemingly brightening up a little bit, she said, "I would love a cup of coffee." Some early morning needs, like coffee, seem to run in our family. Now Mom's request seemed fairly straightforward and relatively simple as I was used to making and drinking a pot of coffee nearly every day at home. I could not have been more mistaken.

My mom's coffee pot was to become a unique exercise in learning for me. She had one of those pots that brews a single cup of coffee at a time. Of course, it also came with a cup in which you could use your own coffee and brew the coffee exactly as you wanted it. As could be expected, this pot came with its own set of "Mom" instructions which I did not know, had not been informed of and which were not written down anywhere. "Don't use a whole portion of coffee and only about two-thirds of the water," were the very explicit and simple instructions emanating from Mom's bedroom.

After looking at the coffee pot, the individual coffee maker, and trying to follow Mom's instructions, it was clear that there was a special "key" necessary to make this thing work, and it also appeared I was suddenly incompetent to understand. It is especially embarrassing to be bested by a coffee pot. So in fear of appearing to be an idiot, I went into Mom's bedroom and asked her, "How do you make the coffee pot work?" Of course, what followed thereafter was in that motherly tone of voice as if wondering how I managed to dress myself in the morning. Mom explained the intricacies and nuances of how her coffee pot worked.

After Mom took the time to explain the nuances of her coffee pot, how much water to use, how much coffee to use, she then further instructed me that when the pot was done brewing, "You need to add hot water to the cup." It was not until I brewed the first cup of coffee that I then understood what exactly her instruction for the addition of water meant. When the coffee was done brewing in accordance with Mom's instructions, the cup was no more than one-third full of "coffee."

The coffee that had brewed into the cup had the appearance and consistency of tar. It really looked like if you did not drink the coffee while it was still hot, you would have to have a spoon to get it out of the cup. You had to add water to the freshly brewed sludge to get something that looked more like a normal cup full of coffee. The notion of a home recipe for espresso came to my mind as an explanation of the complex method by which my mom brewed her "coffee." "Why would you not add all the water to start with?" was the question that I wanted to ask so badly but was left unasked. I still, to this very day, do not know the answer to that question.

For the remainder of that first day, I stayed with Mom at her house. I really wanted to be there for her if she needed anything. Not once did she ask me for anything the entire day. She spent the remainder of the morning and most of the afternoon in bed where she spent most of her time watching television.

There was no room or place to sit and even watch television with her. So I pretty much left her to her own devices for the remainder of the day. I was there if she needed me. I knew she was taking naps off and on during the day because periodically, I could hear her snoring throughout the day.

As the day wore on and it became close to supper time, I finally asked Mom if she thought she could get out of bed if I made her dinner. She almost immediately perked up at that suggestion and said she would like that. We spent a few minutes discussing what she would like to have for dinner. She informed me that it had been "a long time since I had a good steak." So steak it was. I told Mom that I would go to the store, buy some steaks; and since my brother would probably be there, I would make a steak dinner for all of us. As I left for the store, Mom actually sounded excited when she said, "I am really looking forward to this meal."

On the way to the grocery store, I decided to make a nice and complete meal for her. I wanted to make her a meal like she always enjoyed getting at a restaurant with my dad. So the plan came together, and we would have our evening special dinner with a good salad, baked potato, and a nice vegetable. The final menu item fit the bill of a nice steak. I picked out some very nice fresh-cut beef tenderloin filet steaks and decided to serve the steak with twice baked potatoes, asparagus with hollandaise sauce, and a fresh garden salad. When I got home and told Mom what the menu was going to consist of, she was unsure "if I can eat all of that, but I will try." Little did mom, or anyone else, realize this steak dinner would be her last "real meal."

When I got back from my trip to the grocery store, but before I had a chance to start dinner, Mom had gotten herself out of bed into her wheelchair without needing any help and had gone to the bathroom. She had then "wheeled" herself into the kitchen where I was sitting at the kitchen table. It was the same kitchen table our family had eaten meals at for many years. It was also the same kitchen table at which Dad had collapsed all those many years before.

Mom started to talk about all kinds of things and about all kinds of topics none of which seemed really very connected as a single train of thought. Some of the things she was talking about made some sense to me while other things she talked about were things that I really knew nothing about. Friends of hers that had taken trips that she was sorry she missed was a pretty frequent topic. Suddenly, her focus shifted to something she said that she had been given while at the hospital for her last pre-procedure examination.

CHAPTER TEN

Mom began to share her story with me. Mom said, "I was sitting in the waiting room at the doctor's office. I really wasn't paying any attention to the folks around me," she said. "All of a sudden, this young girl that I had never seen before and did not know came up to me and said she had something she thought I needed and that she wanted to give to me," Mom continued. "Of course, I asked her what it was that she wanted to give me. Reaching into her pocket, this little girl handed me a small plastic bag. You know, one of those little ziplock sandwich bags that you put sandwiches into." Obviously, this story had piqued my interest, so I asked mom, "Well, what was it she gave you?"

Mom held out her hand which had a firm grip on a little plastic zip-lock bag. She opened the bag and emptied a small wooden cross into her hand. Mom very carefully handed the small wooden cross to me. She told me that the little girl told her, "This is made from a tree that has been at the bottom of a lake for over 100 years. My church pulled the tree from the water and made a bunch of these crosses from the tree. I just felt that you needed one of these crosses." Mom's eyes were actually a little teary as she related this story to me.

She handed me that cross and said, "Take a look at it. What do you think?"

To say that I was dumbfounded would be an understatement. Here my mom was asking me, straight to my face, what I thought about a gift of a wooden cross, and I was worried about what I was going to say to her regarding salvation. The door could not have been any more open than it was at that exact moment in time. It was obvious, given my prolonged hesitation to bring up the subject of my mom's salvation, that someone other than me was holding the door wide open. Yet I was still afraid to go through the door.

I still was not sure what she expected me to say in response to her "what do you think" question. I took the cross from Mom's hand and ran my fingers over it. It was surprising at how smooth the wooden cross was. I continued to hold the cross, feeling its smoothness, for several moments. Then somewhat hesitantly, I put the cross back in the plastic bag and handed it back to Mom. When I handed the cross back to her, I made some remarkably weak comment like, "That is really nice."

Mom took the bag containing the wooden cross back from me and said the wooden cross had "pretty much" not been out of her hand ever since the little girl had given it to her. I made another weak comment "it can't hurt to hang on to it." Her response kind of surprised me; and as I write this, I now fully understand that her next comment could be directed to all of us.

When Mom took the cross back, she said to me, "Oh, I plan on hanging on to it." Once again, the door had been opened to discuss her salvation. I could have walked right in, sat down, and espoused all the information I had regarding salvation. Did I? Ashamedly, no, I did not.

When my mom made her comment about hanging on to her wooden cross, I thought back to the previous night when I was wondering how to talk with her about salvation. Now, it appeared that the opportunity to discuss her salvation was being handed to me on a silver platter.

I wondered about my mom's relationship with Jesus Christ. I wondered if there was, in fact, any relationship between my mom and Jesus. I had never forgotten nor truly understood her outburst when I had asked Dad about his relationship with Jesus all those years ago.

When I heard the next words out of my mom's mouth, I think you could have knocked me over with less than a feather. Apparently, at least to me now while I write this, someone was tired of my constant hesitation to speak to my mom about salvation. I was no longer being allowed the opportunity to consider talking with my mom about salvation but rather was being directly challenged to speak of salvation to her. Now after all those years, after her yelling and becoming very mad at me for asking my dad about his relationship with Jesus, my mom looked directly at me, after some twenty-seven years and said, "What did you mean when you asked your father about his relationship with Jesus?"

I was stunned. There it was, the opportunity to speak to my mom about having a personal relationship with Jesus Christ, the chance to speak with her about her salvation. For more than a few moments, I still was not sure how to respond. Why was she asking me this question? I even had the thought of "was she now 'testing' me?" Was she somehow trying to lay the groundwork for another outburst of anger that I had been the target of when Dad was in the hospital or what? Again, now in retrospect, it is amazing how Satan attacks us in any way possible. There I was, directly faced with the opportunity to share salvation with my mom, and all I was thinking about was how could things go wrong in doing so.

We were sitting at that kitchen table, the same kitchen table where my dad had collapsed before he died. Mom and I had never talked about this issue since the day of my dad's death. Now, Mom was asking me, basically in my own words, what I meant by that question to my dad those many years before. I was unsure of what to say next (Luke 21:14–15, Matthew 10:19–20).

I took a deep breath, swallowed hard, and said, "Jesus Christ said that if we confess Him before our fellow man that He would confess us before His Father in Heaven" (Matthew 10:32) I went on to say that "I believe that this means we have to confess Jesus before each other and outwardly." I then continued by saying, "I also believe that the only way for us to be assured of an eternity in heaven is to accept, or to have accepted, Jesus as our personal Lord and Savior" (John 14:6). I continued with "once we have accepted Jesus Christ as our Lord and Savior we are compelled as children of God to spread the Good News of salvation through that belief and acceptance of Jesus Christ as our Lord and Savior" (Luke 16:15–16).

Mom looked at me and did not say a word. She didn't get upset or mad as I thought she might. There was just absolute silence that seemed to last for many minutes, but I know it really could have been no more than a few seconds.

During that silence, I really did not know what to think. The only thought that was going through my mind was, *Great, now I have done it again. She is going to get mad at you and will probably throw you out of her house.* I honestly thought, after everything else that had brought my mom and me to this point, that her getting upset or mad was actually going to happen. I obviously had placed all my trust in me and forgotten about trusting the Lord (Nahum 1:7).

The most surprising to me was the tone of Mom's voice when she next spoke. There was a somewhat imploring tone in which she asked, "Well, how does that work?"

"How does what work?" was my brilliantly insightful response.

"How does one accept Jesus Christ as Savior?" she asked me.

There I was again, faced with the most important question anyone had ever asked me before; and not wanting to sound like I did not know what I was talking about, I said, "Well, first you must admit that you are a sinner and that as a sinner you are not entitled to salvation through any kind of works or efforts you have made. Then you must acknowledge that only through the forgiveness offered by Jesus Christ and by His shed blood can your sins be forgiven and washed away." I closed my short synopsis of salvation by saying, "Then you must repent from your sinful life and ask Jesus to come into your heart and life as your Savior."

"But I used to go to church every week," was mom's response.

"I know," I said, "But it is not going to church that saves you. It is only through a confession of belief in and acceptance of Jesus Christ as your Savior that you are saved" (John 14:6). I was really pretty sure that my mom was just about "blown out of the water" by what I was telling her. I was equally as sure that she had never been told what I had just told her. Remaining somewhat leery, even at this point, that Mom would get angry at me for saying these things to her, I continued to share the Good News with her. No such outburst ever occurred.

We sat at the kitchen table for the better part of an hour. During that time, the only topic of conversation was about Jesus and his offer of salvation and forgiveness of sins. Mom kept saying things like, "But I have always tried to be a good person." In confirmation of my belief that Mom had never heard that Jesus was the only way and the only path to salvation, she asked me, "Why did my church never talk about things of salvation?" I could not answer that question for her at that time. She finally changed the topic and began to be more inquisitive into what was going to be the dinner plans. I then told her to hang onto her wooden cross, and I would go ahead and get dinner ready.

I guess I was thinking that somehow with Mom continuing to hold onto that little wooden cross, doing so would keep her heart open to be moved to a point of confession of faith and belief in Jesus Christ as her Savior. That was my prayer at the time. Whatever the reason, the little wooden cross was never out of her hand again. Mom even continued to hold onto the wooden cross as we went ahead and had our dinner that evening. I now believe that God was most certainly working in Mom's heart. I only hoped that when God had finished his work in Mom's heart, I could be there when she accepted Jesus Christ as her Lord and Savior.

CHAPTER ELEVEN

The next day was Friday; and early that morning, even before I had a chance to make coffee for her, Mom called me to her room. When I got there, Mom said that she was in a little pain and that her "right side hurt like maybe I cracked a rib in a coughing bout during the night." I asked her what the pain felt like (as if I could do anything about it). "Feels like a strong twinge," was the only way she could describe it.

So once again resorting to the old hospital pain rating system, I asked her how she would rate the pain on that scale. "Oh, only about a one or a two," was her response.

"Well," I said, "you do have your pain medications here if you need to take some."

"I know", she said. "But I really don't like what the pain medication does to me. Maybe if I just lie on the heating pad, that will help." "I am going to try that first," was the end of that brief conversation. I left Mom to the heating pad with the hope that it would provide her with at least a little pain relief. I headed to the kitchen to make some coffee. During the rest of that Friday morning, Mom stayed in bed and continued lying on her heating pad. She watched television; and as I checked with her periodically, she dozed off and took short naps off and on for almost the entire morning.

At lunch time, I asked mom what she wanted for lunch. "A glass of orange juice," was her reply. I asked if that was all she wanted. She said that it really was and then added, "I really don't feel really hungry." It was only later that my brother told me that a glass of orange juice was her typical lunch fare. I think that if I had left her to her own devices, she would not have eaten even that much.

That Friday afternoon was virtually an exact copy of what transpired on Friday morning. Mom stayed in bed, lying on the heating pad in her attempt to make the pain go away. The only time she changed positions was when she had to get up and go to the bathroom. For whatever reason, Mom would not let me help her get into her wheelchair. But after she managed to get herself situated in the wheelchair, she would let me help push her down the hall to the bathroom and back into her bedroom afterward. She would let me help her get back into bed and then make sure she had water and could get her pain pills if she needed them. Beyond that, there was very little for me to do as Mom spent the afternoon just resting while continuing to lie on the heating pad.

As it came close to dinnertime that afternoon, I asked Mom what she would like to have for dinner. She told me that her menu selections were "a piece of toast with just a little peanut butter on it." I told her that she really needed to eat more than that but was informed that, "I really don't feel all that hungry."

"Do you ever eat more than a piece of toast with peanut butter on it?" I asked.

"Oh, if Rob comes over after he is done working, he fixes me something," she said. Later on, when I asked Rob what type of things he made for mom, "something" more often than not turned out to be Marie Callender's frozen dinners that my brother popped into the microwave for their joint dinner. Mom told me that the only reason she ate that much was because Rob had also told her that she needed to eat more than she was.

So I made Mom her peanut butter and toast for which she did manage to come to the table to eat. After her "dinner," she got up from the kitchen table, got herself back into her wheelchair, and made another excursion to the bathroom. While Mom was in the bathroom, I heard her moan as if she was in a great deal of pain and needed help. "Are you okay in there?" I asked.

"Yeah, I am okay right now," was her reply.

When Mom came out of the bathroom, I asked her what was wrong. She told me, in the kindest terms possible, that the "whole process of going to the bathroom was very painful." I asked her if she could identify where it did hurt and she said, "Right at that spot where I have had pain all day." I told her that if the pain got any worse, she should take some of her pain medication and go back to bed. Agreeing with that suggestion, she wheeled herself down the hallway to her bedroom. While she was doing that, I got her a glass of water so she could take her pain medication.

When I got to her room with the glass of water, Mom was already back in bed. She asked me to make sure her heating pad was plugged in as she said, "I think I caught the cord in my wheelchair."

Finding that the heating pad was plugged in, I asked Mom, "Where is your pain medication?"

"In my dresser drawer," she said. I have to admit with her dresser being completely unreachable from her bed, this seemed like an unusual spot for her to keep her medications and in particular her pain medication.

I think Mom saw the quizzical look on my face when she volunteered, "I keep it there so that I have to make a strong effort to get it and to make sure I really need it." Now that is some maternal logic that you cannot argue with. Mom's pain medication was not a new prescription as a result of the current issues she was facing but rather was some oxycodone she had left over from her last brain surgery. She took one of the tablets and was asleep by 7:00 p.m., and Friday was over for Mom. I went to bed a little later and, before falling asleep, spent some time thinking about what the next day would bring for both of us in this process.

It was quite early the next morning, Saturday being a day that I usually liked to sleep in, but I heard Mom already awake. I also heard that Mom was in the bathroom once again. Again, it was quite obvious that she was in a great deal of pain as I could hear her moaning in the bathroom. "Are you okay?" I asked through the closed door.

"I am really hurting," was her reply.

"Do you need me to come in there and help you?" I asked.

"No, I will be out in a minute," was her response.

When mom finally came out of the bathroom, I asked her, "What and where is it really hurting?"

"My side is bothering more today than it did yesterday," was her surprising answer. Mom had not really complained specifically about her side before. I then asked her how she would rate the pain. "Oh, it is probably about 5 or 6 this morning. I was really hurting in the bathroom," was her worrisome reply.

I told Mom that we were going to be keeping a very close eye on her pain level. I also told her that if her pain got any more severe, we were going to head for the hospital to have her checked out. Mom assured me that if her pain got any worse, she would gladly go to the hospital. It was at that point that I learned just how much pain Mom was in. As much as I tried at that point, I could not convince Mom to let me take her to the hospital at that time so she could get checked out and to determine the cause of her pain.

All she said to me was that she was going to take some more pain medication and lie back down on her heating pad. "Brent, could you bring me some water so that I can take my pain medication?" was her only question to me. So I got her a glass of water and handed her a pain pill. She took the medication, swallowed most of the water, and was asleep on top of her heating pad within a matter of minutes.

I let Mom rest and did not wake her for the rest of that morning. I was very confident that if she needed anything, she would wake up and call me. There really was very little for me to do other than to be there if she needed anything. I spent most of the rest of the morning watching television, reading a little, and did a lot of thinking.

A lot of my thinking that Saturday morning was over the many past years that had been wasted by both my mother and me as a result of all the things that had transpired over those years, beginning with the issue of my dad's death and me asking about his salvation. That issue, combined with many other things that I had done over the course of the ensuing many years, had led to my mother and I having little if any type off mother-son relationship. I could not seem to get those thoughts out of my head. Again, the source of the causation of this breakdown in our relationship had primarily been my fault but which now, without knowing how much time mom had left, seemed like such a waste of time and had been so senseless.

Because of and as a result of all these feelings and thoughts, I had a strong feeling that now that my mother was in such bad physical health and that there was no way of knowing what her remaining time may be, there was little time to make some sort of amends between us. It seemed so silly that neither of us, but especially me, had made little if not no effort to heal the hurt that I was the major contributor to and which had kept us apart.

I also spent time thinking about Mom's pain and how it seemed to be getting worse rather than getting any better. I renewed my thoughts that perhaps we should really be thinking about whether, or not we should get Mom back to the hospital or call the doctor for his recommendation. I finally made the decision that if her pain got any worse that morning or that afternoon, I would call my brother, Rob, and suggest to him that we take mom back to the hospital to see why her pain was increasing.

About midafternoon on that Saturday, after mom had spent all morning and the early afternoon asleep on the heating pad, Mom woke up and very loudly complained that her side was really hurting her. "So where would you rate the pain now?" I asked.

She said that the pain was "about a 7 or 8." Now it seemed the pain was getting worse even after having taken some pain medication. Mom asked me to help her to the bathroom. I helped her into her wheelchair and rolled her down the hall.

It was only moments after Mom got herself into the bathroom that it became abundantly clear the pain was getting worse. When Mom came out of the bathroom, she told me that not only did she have side pain but that it had gotten to the point that in her effort to relieve her pain, her pain medication now seemed to be making it difficult for her to go to the bathroom.

While wheeling her back to her room, I asked Mom to tell me more about her side pain. She told me, "It is getting worse." One more time, I asked her about where she would rate her pain. She now told me that she would rate her pain as "It is at least a 9 if not a 10." I asked her if she wanted to go to the hospital right then. When she said she did not want to go, I reminded her that we had agreed that if the pain got any worse, we were going to the hospital. We then agreed that she would take another pain pill, go back to bed; and if the pain was the same in the morning, we are going to the hospital. Mom said she was okay with that plan. Again, when she told me that she would go to the hospital in the morning if her pain was no better, I knew that her pain was worse than she was telling me. Mom got back into bed, turned the heating pad back on, took another pain pill, fell asleep on the heating pad, and did not stir until the next morning.

Sunday morning began with quite clear and obvious evidence that we would be making a trip to the hospital. Mom woke up with such intense pain that she could not even get out of bed. At her request, I again got her a glass of water so she could take her pain pill. When I took the water to Mom, she said, "I hurt so bad that I don't even want to get up." So again, trying to get some true indication of how bad her pain was, I asked her to again rate the pain for me. "It's at least a 10," she said. I knew that it had to really be hurting because Mom had never really been one to complain of pain. If she said it was a 10, I knew it had to be even more painful than that.

It was not too long after Mom took her pain medication that my brother showed up at the house. For whatever reason, Rob was not in a very good mood when he came to the house for his usual morning visit to see how Mom was doing. I was about to make his morning even worse.

CHAPER TWELVE

Not wanting to talk in front of mom, I took Rob into the living room. I explained to him about how Mom had been taking pain pills fairly regularly while complaining about the increase in how much paid she was having. I also told Rob that Mom had rated her pain that morning as at least a 10.

I made the suggestion to Rob that we should go ahead and take Mom to the hospital to have her pain complaint checked out and to see what, if anything, could be done to alleviate or at least reduce her pain. After a brief and understandable cussing episode to vent his frustration and then his concern for Mom's condition, he agreed that we should get her ready to go and get her into the car for yet another trip to Rochester to see the doctors.

Rob had made it sound like getting Mom ready to go to the doctor was going to be a major undertaking. It really turned out not to be all that difficult to get Mom dressed and ready to go. All we had to do was to get her out of her pajamas (at her request) and into some sweats so that she would at least feel comfortable in public.

As we were getting ready to leave the house, Mom asked, "Where is my wooden cross? I want to have that with me." At that moment, I was deeply touched by her request or demand, as it may be, to have her wooden cross with her. I am not sure I had given any thought to her wooden cross had she not been so adamant to have it with her.

I went into her bedroom, found the wooden cross in her bed where she obviously had been sleeping with it. I took it back to the front door and handed the cross to Mom. "Thank you," she said and actually tightly clutched the small wooden cross close to her chest. It would not be the last time I saw Mom clutching that small wooden cross close to her chest over the next few days.

I must admit there was a little struggle getting all of Mom's oxygen tanks and so forth into the car and then getting Mom into the car. The bending and twisting it took for Mom to get into the car seemed to cause her a good deal of pain. Once she was in the car, we were then able to get her oxygen reconnected, and we set off for Rochester and to St. Mary's Hospital.

When we arrived at St. Mary's, we took Mom directly into the emergency room lobby, got her checked in, and then began the waiting to be seen by one the physicians on duty. It was Sunday, May 29, 2011, and none of us knew what was in store for us over the course of the next several days.

With the usual expectation of a somewhat lengthy wait to be seen in the emergency room, we settled in for what I was afraid would be a somewhat long wait. Rob went outside to have a cigarette, and Mom was sitting in a wheelchair right next to me. I really hoped the wait would not be too long as the chairs were as uncomfortable as is the seating typical of most emergency waiting rooms.

We had only been sitting in the emergency waiting room for a few minutes, when all of a sudden, Mom literally doubled over in the wheelchair, with her chest actually touching her thighs and let out a long and loud moan.

I was quite startled by this, and I asked Mom, "What's the matter?"

"The pain is unbearable," she replied between gasps.

"How bad is it?" I asked.

"It must be at least a 14 or 15," was her answer. Clearly out of the proverbial scale of 1 to 10, it was obvious that what Mom felt was hurting her with excruciating pain. Mom continued to moan and now began to slowly rock back and forth while she moaned. I felt helpless sitting there while Mom was in such pain. All the while, Mom had her fist tightly clenched around the little bag that was holding her small wooden cross.

It was not very long after Mom's spasm of intense pain that Mom, along with Rob, who had returned from his smoke break, and me were taken into an examination room. In a matter of only minutes after we were taken into the exam room, the resident on call arrived and began her examination of Mom. When the resident asked Mom what her chief complaint was, Mom told her of the intense pain and when it began. Mom then asked if she could have something for the pain right away and to stress that point ended her request with a strident, "I mean right now!"

The resident was very attentive, sympathetic, and was really listening to mom's complaints and her less-than-subtle demand for pain medication. The resident then actually ordered some immediate pain medication. In addition, she also ordered the lab tests and blood work necessary to try and determine what was causing Mom's extreme pain and why it had gotten so bad so suddenly. The resident then left the exam room and thereby left the three of us there looking at each other as no one said a single word.

Not long after the resident left the exam room, the lab tech came in to draw the first set of blood work and so forth that had been ordered. Shortly after the lab tech had finished her work, the resident returned and informed the three of us that Mom was going to be taken for a CT scan of her pelvis and abdomen. This news upset Mom quite a bit as she stated that she did not think that a CT scan was really necessary. At that point, none of us really understood why a pelvic CT scan was necessary, and honestly I don't think any of us thought to ask why.

However, Mom knew that if the doctor ordered the test, she would have to go without complaining anyway, not that that stopped her from complaining anyway. But even over her complaining, off she went for her CT examination when the orderly came to take her to the imaging lab.

Just before Mom left the examination room, the nurse tried to get Mom to leave the small wooden cross with my brother and me. Mom would not let the nurse take the small wooden cross from her, and finally the nurse gave up her efforts to take the cross from Mom. Rob and I were then left to wait in the examination room. Not only were we left alone physically, we were also left alone with our own individual thoughts. We both sat there very quietly and stared at the walls, saying very little, if anything at all, to each other for the entire time Mom was gone.

Much to my surprise, Mom was returned to the examination room in a little less than one hour. At the time, I thought that was quite surprising and had been a relatively short time to get her in and out of the CT lab and back to the exam room.

I had made the decision that while Mom was gone to the CT lab that I would call Mom's church and ask the secretary at the church to inform Mom's pastor that we were at the hospital in Rochester. I also wanted to see if perhaps Mom's pastor could come to the hospital for a few minutes to see Mom.

It was not too long after I made the call to inform Mom's church and pastor that we were at the hospital that I got a call back from Mom's pastor asking me what was happening. I shared some of the details of the past couple of days with her and filled her in on where we were, what testing was taking place, and so forth. The pastor asked if we would like her to come over and be with us. I told her that Mom had previously indicated that she would like for the pastor to be at the hospital if that was possible.

The pastor said she would "finish up a couple of things" that she still had left to do after Sunday service and that she would be on the way over immediately after that. I reminded her that we were actually in the emergency department; and that if anything changed before she got there, I would be sure to let her know.

It was shortly after I finished my telephone call with the pastor when Mom was rolled back into the examination room. She was already finished with all of the tests and CT scans that had been ordered. Now all we had to do was to sit, wait, and try to be patient as we awaited the results of the CT scan and all the other tests. It probably goes without saying that while we were waiting, Mom was subjected to more blood samples being drawn and additional lab tests being ordered.

It had gotten to the point that Mom sarcastically asked if she "could just donate a pint all at once so you don't have to stick me anymore?" I know that she did not like having all the needles poked into her; and for a moment, the sarcastic humor of her question somewhat lightened the mood present in the examination room.

Part of that "request" regarding blood being taken was Mom's sarcastic sense of humor arising in a time of trouble for her. However, the truly physical part of the pain in having multiple blood draws was the fact that Mom had such fine veins that it was difficult for techs to get a good vein from which to draw blood. Oftentimes, in the past as the story was related to me, lab techs would give up in frustration after making several attempts to locate a vein from which they could actually draw a blood sample. There had been one occasion when the lab tech actually called a physician to help in her attempt to find a useable vein from which to draw a sample of Mom's blood.

Once the lab tech had made what we were told would be the last blood draw and left the examination room, the waiting began anew, wait and then wait a little more. That was all we could do between nurse visits and vital signs checks. While we were waiting, Mom decided she wanted to talk about the "what ifs" with us. She asked Rob and I, "What if they find more cancer?"

Clearly, this was her greatest fear. Rob and I both said, "Well, let's not jump to conclusions and just wait and see what the doctor says." Neither of us could think of anything else to say. What can you say at a time like that? What thoughts could either of us offer that would erase such a clear, deep, and manifest fear?

The lack of any real meaningful response from neither my brother nor me did anything to curb Mom's obvious concern, fear, and anxiety. She was very clearly thinking about the potential and ultimate progress of the cancer that was in her. It also soon became equally obvious that she was thinking about the full brain scan radiation treatment that was supposed to start on the following Tuesday.

Bringing that issue into play arose when Mom said, "I don't know if I want to go through any full brain radiation treatment if they find more cancer."

"Well," in a really weak response to Mom's concerns, I offered, "let's just wait and see what the doctor says. Maybe she can give us some idea of what the plan might be."

"It seems like that brain radiation treatment would be a waste of time," she continued.

"Mom, all we can do is to wait and see what we learn," was my remarkably feeble response.

All three of us kind of expected a long wait given that we were in the emergency room on the weekend. We felt this was especially true as we waited for what we thought would be a long time for the results of the CT scan. I guess the one good thing about being in the St. Mary's emergency department was that all of Mom's medical records were there. As we later learned, and a second good thing, was the fact that the oncology department had staff on call and in the hospital even on weekends. In addition, there were people on site who would be able to read and interpret the CT scans. Even having become informed of all this information, I was still a little surprised at how fast we would eventually learn the results of Mom's test.

The emergency room attending physician came into the examination room. I don't know how anyone else felt about his body language, but I sure got an ominous feeling which did not seem to bode well for mom. "Mrs. Johannsen, I am the attending physician," he said. "We will keep you comfortable here while we wait to hear the final results of your CT scans. If there is anything you need, you just let me know. How are you feeling right now? How is your pain level?"

Mom wasted no time in telling him, "Well, I am still waiting for something to take away the pain."

"I will have something brought into you right away," was his response. The he asked, "Hasn't anyone brought you anything since you have been here?"

"No, not yet, and I am really hurting," was mom's strained and strident response.

The attending physician left the exam room; and within a matter of moments, a nurse was in the examination room, providing Mom with some of her requested pain medication. I am not sure what the pain medication was, but it was not long before Mom said, "Oh, that feels so much better." Once again, the three of us returned to our waiting game, anxious for any word about Mom's CT scans.

Soon the resident that first saw Mom came into the examination room. Her outward demeanor appeared to me to be even more foreboding than that of the attending physician had been. "We have the CT results," she stated bluntly, matter-of-factly, and with some apparent difficulty. "You have a new tumor on your liver, and you appear to have a lesion on your T-6 vertebrae. We think that it is the lesion on your vertebrae that is causing your pain. We are going to send the scans up to the oncology department for their review to see if the preliminary reading is accurate," was her final diagnostic statement.

The resident then asked Mom, "Is your pain level under control now?"

"Yes, it is," was Mom's very quiet and equally subdued response. "What is the plan now?" Mom asked.

"Well, we will keep you comfortable here while we wait to hear what the oncology department suggests we do for you," replied the resident. "We may want to keep you in the hospital for a little while. It just depends on what oncology says."

"Okay," was all the response Mom could muster. I believe that both Rob and I were stunned into silence with this new information and dreadful diagnosis.

It was not long after the diagnostic disclosure of the resident had been delivered to us that the attending physician again came into the examination room. He then disclosed the entire diagnostic readings of the CT scan that we had just received. "Do you need any more pain medication?" was the only question he asked Mom. When mom replied that she was okay for now, he again said, "Well, if you need anything, be sure to let us know." With that statement, he left the examination room, and we never saw him again.

CHAPTER THIRTEEN

With three of us in the examination room, it was remarkably quiet. I really believe you could have heard the proverbial pin drop. Mom lay on the gurney, kind of just looking off into space. I sat in a chair across the room from her. Rob chose to stand in the corner. I really felt sorry for him as he looked like he was doing everything in his power to keep from crying in front of us. I know for a fact he was not alone in those feeling.

None of us seemed to know what to do or what to say. I mean, what do you, or could you say in a situation like this? I watched Mom's hand go up in the air as she was holding her small wooden cross in her hand. She held the small wooden cross up where she could see it. She then clenched that hand over her other hand and lowered them both to her chest. I believe at that point Mom was praying. Whether for comfort, peace, strength, or healing, I do not know. She never said a word while she did that. Rob, on the verge of tears, left the room.

A short while later, the resident returned with Rob, close on her heels, following her right into the room. The doctor asked Mom if she needed anything. "Yes, I do," she said. "I know you are not an expert. I know that anything you tell me would be an educated guess, but I want to know what do you think my chances really are?" There was that pin-dropping deafening sound again. Stunned, we all stood there, including the resident, in absolute silence again, for what seemed like many minutes but could not have been more than a few seconds.

"I really am not in a position to tell you that information," replied the resident who seemed to be caught off guard with that question. "I am not holding you to anything you say, but I just want an idea," probed mom. The resident looked at all of us, took a deep breath, and offered, "Well, we think you have anywhere from three weeks to a couple of months."

Now we were enveloped in an even more deafening silence. "Three weeks to a couple of months" was a death sentence that I don't think any of us was ready to hear. It was almost incomprehensible. It was a period of time that seemed like it would be here before we were ready for it to be here. The resident left the room without saying anything else. Rob stood a few more minutes in the corner, burst into tears, and ran out of the room.

He had been with Mom at her beck and call for many months, and this news clearly overwhelmed him. I sat back down and slumped in the chair. I was completely stunned at the speed with which things had spiraled downhill in such a relatively short time and now, even more so, seemingly out of control.

With Rob gone out of the room, I was in the examination room alone with Mom. She looked at me, fighting back her tears and losing that battle, she began to cry. "So what do I do now?" she asked as she looked at me with huge tears in her eyes. She seemed to be almost begging me for an answer. "I don't know. I don't know," was all I managed to get out between my own efforts to not break down in tears and run out of the room like Rob had done.

"Well, I don't think I am going to go ahead with the full brain radiation treatments," was mom's first comment after she had finished crying for this moment. "Seems like a waste of time to me" she continued.

"Let's wait and see what the oncologist says after he has had a chance to look at the scans," was all I could muster to say. I stood up and went over to the gurney, grabbed Mom's hands that were still holding the small wooden cross, and said, "Just hang on to this," as my effort at consoling her. I really believed that that was all she could do but was unable to find the words to express that thought.

In retrospect, I find that I am ashamed of myself. I had been thinking about how to talk to Mom about salvation and now, with this new despairing news, all I could muster was, "Just hang on to this." Maybe that was enough at the time, but it also did not seem like enough at the time. I believe that, even under those circumstances, I was still afraid of what my Mom would say if I spoke to her about her personal salvation. Not long after this, Mom's pastor arrived at the hospital.

When the pastor came into the room, I think she could tell that things were not going all that well. No one said anything or offered her any information when she first came into the examination room. "Hi, Ann, how are you doing?" was her initial question.

"Not good," Mom said. Pastor looked at me, and I told her the news we had just gotten.

"I am so sorry, Ann," she said to Mom. It was at that point that I thought I would leave the room so that Mom could have some private time with her pastor.

When I returned to the examination room several minutes later, Mom's pastor was involved in some form of what she called a "positive energy" treatment, trying to help Mom feel less pain. I must admit that this form of "treatment" troubled me. I do believe in the scriptural based "laying on of hands" for healing, but what I was witnessing did not fit into the way I understood Scripture. While I had some significant doubts about the source of this "treatment," I made no comment about this "treatment" because Mom did seem to be at least relaxing a little.

Not long thereafter, in fact within a few minutes after the "treatment" ended, the resident came back into the examination room and informed us that she had begun the process of getting Mom admitted to the hospital. She told mom, while the rest of us listened in, that "we need to keep you in the hospital for a few days to see if we can get your pain under control and then maybe we can send you home."

My brother asked, "Would she be staying in the hospital at St. Mary's?"

"No," replied the resident. "She will be going to Methodist Hospital as soon as we can arrange a room for her and transportation to get her over there."

My brother then wanted to know, "How long do you expect all that will take?"

"It shouldn't take too long," was the reply from the resident. "I have already contacted the transfer ambulance service. And when they get here, we should be able to transfer her at that time."

All the while, as this brief conversation between my brother and the resident took place, I was looking at Mom to see her reaction as we were told this information. She did not look very happy about the idea of staying in the hospital for any more time. In fact, she flatly stated, "I really don't want to stay in the hospital." Rob and I both told her that she was going to have to stay in the hospital until her pain was under control. We told her that once her pain was under control, we could then take her home. We all finally did agree that if she was in the hospital, it would give us a chance to talk to the oncologist sooner. With a great deal of displeasure and resignation, Mom finally agreed that it was a good idea for her to stay in the hospital even if she didn't want to.

It ended up taking more than an hour before the transfer ambulance arrived to take Mom to the Methodist Hospital. During that time of waiting for transfer, it became an hour or so where very little of anything was said by any of us. Surprisingly, to me, this even included the pastor who had agreed to stay until the transfer ambulance arrived. I think I at least expected perhaps an offering of prayer for Mom and the family while we waited. No such offer was made. Of course, I could have made the same offer under the circumstances, but I remained silent also. It just seemed like we were a little bit lost and quite unsure of what exactly we should do. So we all just sat there, alone in our own thoughts, waiting for an ambulance.

Finally, the transfer ambulance arrived, and Mom was carefully loaded into the ambulance for her ride to Methodist Hospital. The transfer attendants asked Mom if she would let go of her small wooden cross for the transfer ride. They asked if she would let one of them hold onto the cross for her until she got into her room. Mom refused even that simple request for the short time the transfer ride would take. I must admit that her refusal to surrender her small wooden cross came as a bit of a surprise to me.

I was given the opportunity of riding in the front seat of the ambulance with Mom as we drove to Methodist Hospital. Rob said that he would "meet us at the hospital" as he was going to drive the car we had ridden to Rochester in. I cannot say for certain; but I believe, seeing his face when he did arrive at the hospital, that Rob shed more than a few tears in that short ride. I know I did while I was riding in the front seat of the ambulance. I am thankful that the ambulance driver must have understood the situation as he did not ask any questions or attempt to make any small talk on the drive.

I believe that the ten-minute ride to Methodist Hospital was without a doubt one of the longest rides I have ever taken. I know it was not far and did not take long, but it seemed that time had begun a slow and inextricable march to some undetermined destination point. It was a destination point that I did not know or understand where it was. It was also a destination point that would, in the end, be clearly and meaningfully displayed for all in our family to see.

Once we arrived at Methodist Hospital, the ambulance crew efficiently and quickly got Mom out of the back of the ambulance and immediately into the receiving doors. In fact, I was almost jogging as I followed them down the hallway, to the elevator, then up to the fourth floor where Mom's room was. The transfer crew wheeled Mom into what turned out to be a private room that was actually quite spacious. However, Mom's room had absolutely no view outside of her window, save for the brick wall of the building next door. If you were a contortionist, you could lean way over the left end of the window and manage to catch a peek at the blue sky that Sunday afternoon.

It was not a very cheerful or uplifting room even as far as any hospital room is concerned. Other than the typical hospital fluorescent lights, which were off, the only natural light was a small amount of sunlight that managed to sneak into the room from the space between the two buildings.

With the overhead fluorescent lights off, the room was actually in a sort of continual dusk like lighting. I asked Mom if she wanted me to turn on the overhead lights so there would be a little more light in the room. Mom said that she liked it with the lights off, so the overhead lights were left off during the remainder of the entire day.

The room also had several chairs and a love seat to sit on or sleep in if the need arose.

Within a few minutes of arriving in Mom's room, the ambulance attendants had Mom off of the gurney and transferred to her bed, then picked up their "belongings" and were gone. A nurse was in the room beginning to do all the plugging in that was needed to monitor Mom's vital signs. I was actually quite impressed and somewhat surprised at the speed and efficiency of the nurse as she went about her duties.

A second nurse then entered Mom's room and asked Mom if there was anything she needed. "Yes," was her almost immediate reply. "I am in terrible pain. Can I get some pain medication NOW," she seemingly ordered the nurse to act. I must admit I felt a little embarrassed over the rude way in which Mom had addressed the nurse.

In fact, I actually went out and apologized to the nurse for Mom's reaction. "Not to worry," was the nurses reply. "I am pretty sure that after her travels and getting man-handled into and out of the ambulance and then into the bed that she is in a good deal of pain." Now I was ashamed of myself again because I had not thought about how much pain Mom must have been in with all that moving and shuffling her around.

I was nosy and asked the nurse if she could tell me what pain medication had been ordered, "Your mom will be given morphine to begin with and will continue to be on morphine until we get her pain under control. Once we get the pain under control, we can then work at cutting back on the dosage or changing the medication to something else." I really don't know why I asked about Mom's pain medication, but it seemed like I should know in case anyone else in the family wanted to know.

My brother came into Mom's room shortly after I had finished talking to the nurse about Mom's pain medication. It was all too obvious that he had been crying. I did not say a word to him about his crying as I was dealing with my own similar reaction to the whole situation. Rob told me that he had called his kids, my nieces and nephews, and told them about their grandmother's condition. Rob also told me that "I managed to get ahold of Sarah. She wants to know if she should come now to see mom or wait and see what happens with her treatment."

My sister, Sarah, lives in Germany. To tell her to come right away would be to place a huge burden on her particularly in light of the fact that we were not real sure of Mom's prognosis yet. I asked Rob what he had told her, and he said, "I told her we would discuss it and let her know."

"Probably not a bad idea," was my reply. "It will give us a little time to discuss things with Mom's doctor and see what is really happening and what course of treatment they suggest."

When the nurses left the room, Rob and I sat down to talk with Mom without any thought of what we were going to say or really what the next step was in this process we had just begun. Rob and I just kind of sat in our chairs while Mom lay in her bed; and we all just kind of looked at each other and around the room, not really knowing what to say. I noticed that Mom had another IV started in addition to the one started in the emergency room. She was also now on continuous oxygen and a full-time blood oxygen monitor. Nobody in the room said anything for what again seemed like quite a long time.

Finally, it was Mom herself who broke the silence. "Well, I guess I need to talk to the doctors as soon as possible to see what my next step is."

"What do you want to do?" we asked her.

"If I don't really have a lot of time, I don't want to stay in the hospital if at all possible. I would like to go home and be there until the end."

"Then that is what we will do if it is at all possible," said Rob.

"I guess we will have to wait and see what the doctor says and see if that plan could actually be possible," was my contribution to the conversation. It was a discussion that none of us really wanted to be involved in.

CHAPTER FOURTEEN

I cannot tell you how hard it was to be discussing Mom's imminent death with her. I had never given any thought to the fact that, at some point in time, I could very well be in that conversation, and here I was right in the middle of that conversation. I always thought that when the time came, I would receive a telephone call from Rob or Sarah and would then be told that Mom had passed away. To be actively discussing Mom's death with her was almost unbelievable at the time.

I cannot put into words how weak and helpless it feels to see your Mom dying, to know that, in a matter of only weeks, she would no longer be alive and that there was absolutely nothing you could do about it or anything you can do to change that fact. If you have never been through the process or witnessed a parent's death, all I can tell you is to get ready. When you feel like you should be able to do something about the situation and there is nothing you can do, no matter what the relationship may be with your parent, the feeling of helplessness is almost overwhelming. To sit on the sideline and helplessly watch is nearly unbearable.

As that Sunday afternoon passed, it actually began to be fairly late as we waited with Mom to see a doctor. I truly wondered if a doctor would even be in to see Mom that evening or would we have to wait until Monday morning to get a chance to speak with anyone. I went so far as to even ask the nurse when she came in to check on Mom. "Do you think a doctor will be here to see Mom today, or will we have to wait until tomorrow?" I asked the nurse.

"Oh no," she said. "There will be a doctor in to see her shortly. The oncology attending physician will be here also." I made a very weak "thank you" response as the nurse turned to attend to Mom.

I had barely sat down, and Rob had resumed his emergency room position of leaning on the wall when the oncology resident physician arrived.

The oncology resident introduced herself, and we did the same. She told us that she was an oncology resident and that she would be the one taking care of Mom on a daily basis. She appeared to me as if she maybe had just graduated from medical school, and I wondered to myself how she could possibly be capable of providing care to my mom under these circumstances. I am not sure why I was so negative toward this doctor, in thought at least.

I think I ultimately realized that the negative emotions I felt toward this physician came from my sense of helplessness in the circumstances that existed at that exact moment in time. I guess this sense of helplessness caused my emotions to lead me to question and doubt the obvious ability of this resident. I mean, come on, she was a resident at the Mayo Clinic. I am not sure of how much better treatment we could get. Over the course of the next few days, while watching the overt and genuine concerned care provided by this young resident, I would come to learn that my unfounded concerns were exactly that, unfounded and unnecessary, to say nothing of grossly misplaced.

She said hello to my Mom and told her, "I just need to examine you. Is that okay?"

"Of course," said mom who even tried to smile a little. I really think that Mom was very glad that the physician providing Mom's daily care would be a female. The doctor asked my brother and me if we would mind leaving the room so she could do her examination. It almost felt like both Rob and I could not get out of the room fast enough when we were given this chance.

Rob and I took this opportunity to leave Mom's room, and we went to the family waiting room at the end of the hallway. When we sat down, we started to discuss whether Sarah should come and see Mom now or wait to come and see her when she got home.

"What if she doesn't get home?" was Rob's first question.

"Good point," I said. "If Sarah comes now, she would have a pretty good chance of at least spending some better-quality time with Mom before anything happens," I offered.

"Well, she told me that whenever she comes, she will only be able to stay a week or so," said Rob. "Maybe we should wait and see what the doctors say before we make a decision about what to tell Sarah," I suggested.

"I suppose," was Rob's short and somewhat dejected reply. After a short while of sitting and being lost again in our own thoughts, we finally headed back to Mom's room.

When we got back to Mom's room, the doctor had just completed her examination of Mom. The doctor informed us that when the attending oncologist arrived, she would discuss her examination of Mom with him and review the emergency room notes. After this meeting, they would then come in and talk with us about the results. After telling us this, the doctor told Mom she would see her later and left the room. The next thirty minutes passed in relative quiet, with none of us saying anything.

The next thing we knew, the resident physician and the attending oncologist entered Mom's room. The attending oncologist took the opportunity to introduce himself and told us that he would be supervising Mom's treatment. It was hard not to like him from the minute he introduced himself.

He was a bear of a man with a full black beard. He stood about six feet tall and probably weighed in at close to 250 pounds. Even at that, there really didn't appear to be any excess weight on him. He looked very much like he could have been a professional wrestler as easily as a doctor. He mentioned that he was from a country the name of which I did not hear, but it was very obvious that it was a central European country.

After introducing himself, he told us, "I have reviewed all of the notes, the test results, the CT scans, and the examination notes from the emergency room. It appears that we need to take a real close look at the tests results to make sure we know what we are dealing with here. I will review the tests and examinations with the rest of the oncology department, and tomorrow we will be able to offer you a little better picture of what we are going to be doing to help Mom."

In a strange way, it was somewhat reassuring to me to hear this doctor refer to our mom as "mom" when he spoke of her. "Does anyone have any questions?" he asked.

"I do," said Mom. "Will I be able to go home?" she asked.

"If that is what you want then, that is what we will work toward," was his reassuring answer. We thanked him for his time, and he left the room.

We stayed a while longer with Mom, and there really was very little said by any of us for the rest of the time we were there. "Why don't you both go home and get some rest," mom suggested. Neither Rob nor I said anything to that suggestion. "There really is nothing you can do here, so you might as well go home," was her more forceful implication of what she wanted. I really think Mom wanted us to go home so she could get some rest herself. As if to confirm my suspicion, Mom then said, "I am really tired and think I will just get some sleep now." This comment was voiced in the tone and tenor that indicated to both Rob and I that this was the final directive for us to leave for the night. So at mom's urging, we said goodbye and goodnight to Mom, went out to the nurse's station to leave our contact information, and we then headed home.

The forty-five minutes it took us to drive home from the hospital was pretty much a very quiet trip with both of us seemingly lost in our own thoughts. I am pretty sure neither Rob nor I really knew what to say to each other. Finally, we began to talk about what was happening. "What do you think we should tell Sarah when she calls?" I asked.

"I don't know," was Rob's terse initial response. We again discussed the option of whether Sarah should come right away and maybe spend some "good" days with Mom or should she wait and come when things were not so good or maybe even after Mom had died. We decided, when Sarah called, to tell her exactly what we knew, which was really not that much, and let her decide what she wanted to do. We had therefore arrived at a very good way to dodge the bullet of telling Sarah what to do.

Sunday night was a pretty quiet night. There were times that it was also a pretty desperate night. Rob had talked to Sarah again, and she had decided that she was going to come home as soon as she could get there and then spend whatever time she could with Mom. It was unfortunate that as she was finalizing her plans, it turned out that she would only be able to stay about a week. She would then have to return to Germany.

As Rob and I talked, I think it was generally agreed by all three of us that under the circumstances, Sarah's plan was probably the best resolution of the "come now or come later" decision. Sarah made her final reservations and called us back.

Sarah's plan was that she would be arriving on the coming Friday night and that someone needed to pick her up at the airport in Rochester. Rob said that he had already made plans for Friday night. He had already arranged his schedule so that he could attend his son's high school graduation. He wondered whether, if rather than go to his son's high school graduation, he should pick Sarah up. I told Rob that I would pick Sarah up and that it was important for him to be at his son's graduation.

I told Rob that I would take Sarah straight to the hospital to see Mom right after I picked her up. Rob finally relented and decided that he would attend the graduation ceremony. He then planned on coming to Rochester on Saturday morning to see Mom and Sarah and to spend time with both of them.

Chapter Fifteen

Monday morning dawned; and as I laid in bed, it seemed that the thoughts and events of the previous day had been some sort of dream or more accurately a nightmare. Of course, after a few minutes of time spent waking up, it all sunk in that Mom was indeed in the hospital. Even more emotionally depressing was the fact and realization that Mom had been given only a few weeks to live.

With this ominous realization, I got out of bed, got myself cleaned up, dressed, got a cup of coffee in the hotel lobby, and headed down the interstate to visit Mom in the hospital. As I was driving the short distance to Rochester, I wondered how many times I would be making this trip, how long would it be before Mom was able to go home again, and about what we would do when we were given the various options the doctors may provide us that morning.

Interspersed with each of those thoughts, especially under these new and ominous circumstances, were the multiple, various, and recurring thoughts of, *How do I now go about speaking of salvation with my mom?* Logically it seemed like, under these new circumstances, the issue would be much easier to talk about. However, given the history between Mom and me, I still found myself faced with the same old question of "how do I bring up the subject without making Mom angry at me?" At the time I am writing this, it is almost unbelievable to me that I could remain so concerned and worried about my mom getting mad at me. I am thankful that God is a loving and forgiving God who can excuse my weakness in speaking His truth to my mother.

Seemingly selfish thoughts like those went through my mind when I should have been more concerned with her salvation than with any embarrassment I was afraid of experiencing. I knew that I might not have much of a chance to talk to her about her salvation if I did not do so soon. I realized again, to my chagrin, that I was afraid of this issue, even after her questions at the dinner table just a few days earlier and now particularly in light of her deteriorating physical condition.

In my mind, I knew it was now imperative that I talk with Mom about salvation and what it could and would mean to her. At least I felt like I needed to try and talk with her again. Even with the history between Mom and me, I did not understand why I was having so much hesitation and trouble with the notion of talking to Mom about the greatest news anyone could hear. This was especially true given all of her recent "less than great" news about her medical condition. I was, at that point, unaware of how hard Satan was fighting against my mom being given the opportunity to ensure her eternal salvation and of being in the company of God.

For Mom to hear that God loved her so much as he loves anyone else would be the greatest news I could bring her. To tell her that God loved her so much that He sent his only Son to die a gruesome death on the cross so that she, and everyone else who believed, could be reconciled to God and to then spend all of eternity in heaven would seem like there could be no way for me to be stopped from sharing the greatest news of all time.

Why was I so afraid to bring her this Good News? This was the seemingly never-ending question I was not able to reconcile at the time. The enemy was truly working on me, trying to confuse me, hinder me, and scare me from what I should be doing and saying to mom as she was now facing the greatest test that anyone can have in their life. With my mom on her deathbed, was I not going to tell her about the greatest gift that she could ever receive in this world? It seemed that Satan surely wanted it that way. There should have been nothing keeping me from sharing the message of salvation with my mom. Nothing I may have done in my past should have been preventing me from sharing the Gospel with my mom. Clearly, now it is obvious to me that Satan was doing all in his power to keep me from witnessing to my mom.

Mom was actually sitting up in bed when I got to her room that Monday morning. "How do you feel?" I asked her, which sounded like a really stupid question as it came out of my mouth.

"I still hurt, but they are working on getting my medications under control," was her answer.

"Are they taking good care of you," was my next brilliantly inane question."

Oh, yes, in fact, I really like the nurses I have had so far. They are right here when I call for them, and they seem to be really concerned about keeping me comfortable," she informed me.

I was really glad to hear that Mom liked her nurses. After her initial contact with them when she was first taken to her room, I was a little hesitant, not as to how they would treat Mom but rather as to how Mom would treat them. She was one of those people you hear about that "do not easily suffer a fool" or at least someone she perceived to be a fool. "You know, they actually have a room service menu to order my meals from," Mom said.

"Really," was my quick-witted response. "Have you ordered anything yet?" I asked.

"I was just getting ready to order when you came in," she said.

"Well, don't let me stop you," I told her.

Mom picked up the phone at her bedside, dialed the cafeteria, and ordered herself a breakfast that consisted of black coffee and two slices of crisp bacon. "Are you sure you wouldn't like something more than that for breakfast?" I asked.

"No, I think that is all I really need," Mom replied.

"Well, we don't want you to stuff yourself now," I kidded her. She looked at me and informed me that she really didn't feel like eating any more than that.

While we waited for Mom's "breakfast," we really did not talk about anything of real importance. Mom wanted to know where Rob was that morning, and I told her that he was at work but that he was only a phone call away. "Do you want me to call him and have him come over" I asked.

"No, he needs to stay at home and work," was her quick although not thoroughly convincing response. I asked her again if she wanted me to call him and have him come over. Again, she said no, that he needed to stay home and work; and with that, I let the question drop.

When Mom's breakfast arrived, the smell of the hot coffee overwhelmed the entire room. "Boy, that coffee smells good, doesn't it?" Mom asked.

"Yeah, it does. I probably should have ordered some for myself," I said only half-jokingly.

Mom offered, "I can call back down and have some more sent up."

"No, that's okay. I will go down and get some when they come in to bathe you and take you to the bathroom," I told her.

It was at that very moment when the attending physician then arrived, along with his collection of residents, interns, and medical students, crowding Mom's room and began asking Mom how she had slept the night before. "Not too bad once I was loaded full of pain killers," she offered.

"How are we doing at keeping the pain down?" asked the attending physician.

"Not too bad. And when I do have pain; the nurses are really good about getting me something fast," she responded.

"Well, that is what we want," said the doctor. He continued by saying, "We don't want you to be in any pain so that maybe we can get you home in a few days."

"That would be nice," was mom's response to that held-out hope.

"Well, you just keep up the good work on your end. and we will try to do the same," replied the doctor.

Looking directly at me, the doctor told me, "I am going to examine your Mom now. You are welcome to stay around if you would like."

"No, that is okay. This would be a good time for me to get some coffee."

"See you in a little while Mom," I said as I left the room in search of a large cup of the same good smelling coffee that Mom has had for her breakfast.

I went down to the ground floor of the hospital in search of someplace to get some coffee. I found the hospital coffee shop and snack bar. The snack bar was like a full-service buffet restaurant. The breakfast buffet was still up with scrambled eggs, hash browns, bacon, sausage, and you could get "made to order" omelets or pancakes if you wanted. I was not that hungry although the "spread" was very tempting and was quite appealing if I would have to spend a great deal of time at the hospital. However, that day, I settled for the hot cup of coffee and sat in the dining area to drink it.

While I sat there, alone in my thoughts, I could not help but, yet again, think about how I was going to try and raise the issue of salvation with my mom. I am thankful that God has patience because I am sure that my constant struggle with discussing salvation with my mom was getting old with Him. I also began to realize that maybe it was Satan that was keeping me from talking with Mom about the issue of her salvation. I prayed a little "bullet" prayer and asked God what I should do and for the strength to do it.

Part of my concern, as misguided as it clearly was, was how was I going to raise this issue again in a way that would not make Mom feel as if she really didn't have a chance of going home. I didn't want her to think that I had "written her off." I knew she really wanted to go home for whatever time she may have left. I got no immediate conscious wisdom in answer to my "bullet" prayer. However, I did have a sense of an answer when I got an overriding and compelling urge to go back upstairs and be with Mom. While nothing spectacular or unusual happened when I got back to Mom's room, I felt very glad and comfortable that I had followed the "direction" of the sense I experienced.

When I got back to Mom's room, the nurse had not quite finished getting Mom cleaned up, so I sat down at the nurse's station to wait. While I was sitting there, I realized that the four nurses working the "pod," in which Mom's room was located, were all registered nurses or RNs. For some reason, I thought that it was quite remarkable that all the nurses were RNs. I guess I assumed that the nurse in charge would be an RN, but I also assumed that the other nurses would be LPNs or even nurse's aides. With this realization, it seemed to me to be a pretty good assurance that Mom would actually be receiving competent and skilled nursing care.

While I was waiting to be able to get back into Mom's room, I wondered off down the hallway to the other "pod" located at the opposite end of the floor. There I discovered that all the nurses on the entire floor were RNs. This discovery brought to my mind my favorite old television show about Mobile Army Surgical Hospitals that promised the "best care anywhere." I was then assured that Mom would receive just that. It was a comfort to me to learn of the high level of expertise and the extent of the training of the nursing staff. All of which for some reason provided me with a quite calming effect.

When I left the nursing pods and returned to Mom's room, she was all freshened up and appeared to be in relatively good spirits. She was sitting up in her bed with new sheets and a new hospital gown. She was on oxygen full time, and she seemed to be tolerating that quite well. "How do you feel now that you are all crisp and clean?" I asked.

Never to be one to hide the facts, Mom replied, "I hurt like hell."

"What happened?" I asked. "All of the moving around has made the pain come back," she replied.

Concerned for this new spasm of pain, I asked, "Well, how would you rate your pain?"

"About an 8 or 9," she replied.

"Let me go tell the nurse that you need some pain medication," I suggested.

"Okay," was her only reply.

As I turned to walk out to the nurse's station, the attending oncologist and his students were entering the room. He introduced himself again and said he would like to speak with me when he had finished with his students and their rounds. I was not sure how to take his request to speak with me. But I told him that would be fine, and I would wait to speak with him. He invited me to stay in the room as he spoke with Mom. I accepted his offer to stay.

"Well, Ann, how do you feel today?" he asked.

"Terrible," was mom's quick reply.

"How would you rate the pain?" was his next question.

"About a 9 or 10," she replied. I told the doctor that I was just on my way to the nurse's station to tell them she needed some pain relief medication when he had come into the room. "We will take care of that," was his reply.

"Let me tell you what we think we have going on here," he said again, speaking directly to Mom. "We have looked at the results of the tests, the blood work, and the CT scans that were done yesterday. We think that there may be even more tumors that we need to clearly identify. So we would like to take you downstairs this afternoon for a couple of more tests. Okay?" I believe I actually saw Mom resign herself to the fate that was being laid out before her. She just kind of slumped her shoulders, and her face seemed to have lost its color and slumped just as her shoulders had.

"What for?" was Mom's somewhat terse and noticeably disappointed response.

Given Mom's tone of voice, the doctor was very patient in his response to her, "We would like to know exactly what we are dealing with so that we can better determine what course of treatment we should take so that we can get you home," he responded. "We cannot know for sure how to treat your pain unless we know exactly what we are dealing with. The tests we want to do will help us a great deal with that determination. Okay?"

At this point in the conversation between the doctor and Mom, my brother came into the room. "What's going on?" he asked.

"Let's go down the hall, and I will tell you. That way, the doctor can finish his examination of Mom, and we can talk."

We headed down the hall to the family waiting room. After we had gotten to the waiting room and sat down, I filled Rob in on what the doctor had been saying. Rob was a little unsure if he wanted Mom to be moved and to go through more tests because he knew how much it hurt for Mom to move. We talked some more and discussed the issue for a few minutes. Together we decided that we would leave it up to Mom whether she wanted to have the additional tests done or not.

When we started to go back to Mom's room, the doctor was heading down the hall directly toward us. He stopped us in the hall and told us, "Mom said she would let us do the additional tests. When we get these new tests done and get the results back, we will be better able to determine which way to treat your mom and hopefully devise a plan where we can get mom home as soon as possible."

"Doctor, let me ask you a question," I said. "I know you cannot know anything for sure until you get these new test results, but how accurate do you think or believe the estimation of the potential time remaining for my mom is that was made by the ER doctor?"

"Without looking at the test results, I cannot say for sure, but I believe that the three weeks to a couple of months estimate is probably pretty accurate," was his very disheartening response. I felt like a lead weight had fallen into the very depths of my stomach.

"Okay, I guess we will see what the tests show," I said.

"Okay, talk with you soon," was the doctor's last comment to us as he headed down the hall. I looked at Rob, and we both could not think of anything to say. "Let's go see Mom," Rob finally said.

When Rob and I walked back into Mom's room, she was getting some medication and appeared to be very relieved to be getting something for the relief of her pain. I sat down in a chair, and Rob took up his usual position of leaning against the wall. It was quite obvious to me that Rob was extremely uncomfortable being in the room and was struggling with seeing Mom in this condition. In fact, there were several times over the course of the next couple days that I saw Rob crying while, very unsuccessfully, hiding his tears and his emotions. He had always maintained the façade of male toughness. I am sure he felt weaker if he was seen crying. I wish that I could have thought of something to do or say that would maybe have helped him at that time.

Mom appeared to be more comfortable as the pain medication began to take effect. As it turned out, Rob and I spent that entire Monday with Mom. While it is true that Mom spent quite some time while we were there taking naps, it is also true that Rob and I spent those times Mom was sleeping deep within our own thoughts and saying very little to each other. When Mom was awake, and we did talk, the conversations were seemingly very insignificant and superficial. We seemed to be having discussions about things that did not really seem all that important at the time. We were having discussions and talks that I presumed most families would have about family things, events, and the like. The unique thing about these conversations that Monday morning was that they were discussions and talks that my mom and I never have had before that day. To have Rob included in them with me was also a new and exciting experience.

In retrospect, I am very glad that we even had those "little" talks about nothing. It was the first real face-to-face effort at the re-establishing of a relationship with Mom and me. To be able to take steps toward re-establishing the relationship that I had done so much to harm and destroy, I now look at as a blessing. Rob and I stayed in the room with Mom until nearly time for her to have her dinner. At that time, and yet again, Mom told both Rob and I to go home. She said, "I am really going to eat and then go to sleep." She then added, as if to establish additional emphasis, "I am really tired." Rob and I left her to her dinner and sleep and headed home. As both Rob and I drove our separate vehicles home that late Monday afternoon, I can't speak for Rob, but I know I was deep in thought for most of the trip.

When Rob and I got home, Rob asked me if I thought it would be okay for him to go to work again on Tuesday. I told him that he should go ahead and go to work. I told him that he should go ahead because there really was very little either of us could do other than to be there if Mom needed anything. I also suggested that it would be important for him to work and try to keep his mind focused on that while I would be there to be with Mom.

I then told Rob that if anything happened, I would call him right away. He told me to make sure that I did call him if anything at all happened. He told me that he could get to the hospital in no time at all. As added assurance, he told me, "I can have a pretty heavy foot on the accelerator if I need to."

Shortly after we got home, Sarah called Rob and confirmed her plans that would have her arriving in Rochester on late Friday afternoon from Germany. Rob again brought up his previously made plans for Friday night. He wanted to make sure I would be able to pick up Sarah at the airport. I assured Rob that picking up Sarah would not be a problem.

My mom and my sister had always had a close relationship. They had taken several cruises together and various other trips. Sarah had lived in Germany for many years and had recently been married in our hometown. It was interesting that Sarah and her husband, Wolfgang, had made a special point of coming back to our hometown for their wedding and to be married in the church that Mom attended. I think this was to make Mom feel better more than for Sarah's benefit.

In fact, in reflecting on the fact that Sarah was married in the church, I must admit that I was a little surprised at that event. Sarah had, for as long as I could remember, been adamantly and ardently anti-church, anti-religious, anti-faith and had even gone so far as to tell me once that she didn't believe in sin and that "therefore nobody died for me." That last statement would turn out to be one of great interest as the next few days went by.

CHAPTER SIXTEEN

My arrival at the hospital on Tuesday morning was as uneventful as it could be under the circumstances. I stopped at the coffee shop to get a cup of coffee and then headed up to Mom's room. At that point, the ordinary daily normal was replaced with a much more unsettling "normal." I wondered if there was any possibility of returning to the old "normal" at all.

When I walked into Mom's room, she looked as if the end was very near. She looked so bad to me that I thought I was very lucky to have gotten there when I did. Mom was largely and for the most part pretty much unresponsive when I walked into her room. I tried to say hello to her and got no response. I continued to try and talk with her; and on those few occasions when she was able to respond to me, it was in guttural sounds which really did not make any sense. I thought for sure that the end was near.

I was so convinced of this that I called Rob and told him to leave work and get to the hospital as soon as he could. I also called mom's pastor and told her it appeared that Mom might not make it and, if at all possible, could she come over to Rochester to be with Mom and us, with us particularly if Mom did not recover and passed away.

I do not recall who was the first to arrive, but it was not long before both Rob and the pastor were there. Mom really was not totally aware, if at all, that any of us were in her room. She remained pretty much nonresponsive to any of us when we each called to her. I asked the nurse if the doctor had been in yet this morning. She told me that the doctor had not made his rounds yet that morning. I told the nurse to let the doctor know that I wanted to talk to him before he left. The nurse assured me that she would have the doctor find me when he finished his rounds.

It was only a matter of minutes, after my conversation with the nurse, when the attending, as well as all the residents, interns, medical students and nurses, again appeared in Mom's room. The attending took one look at Mom and, before any of us could say anything, said, "We need to get her pain medication under control. She looks like she is on too much pain medication," and he walked out of the room.

The implications of the doctor's statement became very clear to me. What I had assumed that Mom was almost to the point of dying was, in fact, Mom's incoherence being caused by excessive pain medication. The doctor gave an immediate order for an adjustment and modification of the pain medication that Mom was to receive.

The attending physician's statement and the subsequent order for modification of Mom's pain medication in and of itself seemed to do more to cheer up the atmosphere in that hospital room than had anything in the last several days. At least now we had a firm and definitive reason why Mom was so suddenly groggy and unresponsive. As it turned out, in only a matter of a couple of minutes, the nurse was back in the room administering some new medication to Mom.

As if to bear out the doctor's diagnosis of potential overmedication, it was only a matter of a few minutes after receiving whatever new or corrective medication that had been ordered that Mom began to "wake up." She now realized that we were there with her, and she began talking to us. In about an hour, Mom was acting as if nothing had happened, and she was ready to order her normal breakfast of a cup of coffee and two pieces of bacon. Meanwhile, I began to feel like I had cried "wolf" with what appeared to be a quick recovery from what I had initially witnessed and what Rob, the pastor, and I had witnessed only a short time before.

Not long after the attending physician left Mom's room, he returned to tell us that the medications Mom had been given were well over and above the amount that should have been administered. He further explained that "once we get the medications under control, the goal is to get your mom home and to be there until the end." As bad as that statement sounded, with the certain death knell it contained, it sounded great. It sounded great particularly after having entered Mom's room that morning and not knowing whether she would last the day or not. The doctor then said he would check on Mom later and left the room again.

With all of us there, Rob, the pastor, Mom, and me, we began to talk about Mom being able to go home. We were all excited about the fact that there existed a possibility for Mom to go home even if it was for only a short time. I really believe that it was, in some way, comforting for Mom that there was that possibility of being at home for her last days. I know that she did not want to be in the hospital until the end. She had even gone so far as to say that she did not want to be in a nursing home if it could be prevented.

Shortly after Mom made her disclosure regarding her desire to not be in a nursing home, the pastor said she had other things to do back in Austin and that she needed to leave. She prayed over Mom, held her hand for a brief moment, and then made her exit. As she left, she told us, "If you need anything, let me know." We thanked her and said goodbye. Rob and I stayed with Mom for most of the rest of that Tuesday.

Yet once again, while Rob and I stayed with Mom, the day was filled with little conversation of anything other than what plans needed to be made and implemented if Mom was, indeed, going to be able to go home, even if only for a short while. Mom was very concerned about getting home health care and so forth. She kept saying that she did not want to have to rely on Rob or me to help her with her activities of daily living. Of course, she also was concerned about how much it would cost to have home health care and the other things she would need during the remainder of her time.

After a few more hours, Rob decided to leave for the day. He left that day saying he was going to go back to work. Again, he told me that if anything changed, I was to let him know immediately. With that, he headed out the door and went back to work.

After Rob left, I asked Mom how she was feeling. "I feel pretty good considering everything," was her response. She really appeared to be lost in thought and was a little teary eyed.

"What are you thinking about?" I ventured to ask. I don't know what I expected her to be thinking about under the present circumstances, but the answer she gave me came as a complete surprise to me.

Mom started to cry a little bit and managed to tell me, "I never wanted you kids to go through this."

"Go through what?" I asked.

"Sitting at my bedside while I died," was her short and tearful response.

That answer made me start to well up, ready to cry myself. "I don't want you saying anything like that again," I told her. "We are not going through anything compared to what you have gone through, and you need to just focus on you getting stronger so we can get you home."

Mom and I continued to talk for some time after that. Our conversation was nothing overly serious or meaningful in the grand scope of things. However, in hindsight, it was an opportunity for my mother and I to, in some small way, make an additional effort at restoring our relationship. For that opportunity and given the large part on my behalf in causing the breakdown of our relationship, I am and will be forever grateful.

Neither of us really knew what to say given the enormity and totality of the situation, but at least we were trying. As the afternoon wore on, I could see Mom was getting visibly tired. I told her that I was going to leave and that I would see her in the morning. She said that would be great as she admitted that she was tired and really wanted to go to sleep. I left Mom's hospital room just as Mom actually fell asleep.

CHAPTER SEVENTEEN

The next morning, a bright, sunny Wednesday morning with almost no clouds in the sky, I again made the trip over to Rochester to see Mom. That morning, I made the journey by myself. Rob had decided that he needed to stay in Austin so that he could work. I guess he trusted that I would call him if Mom took a turn for the worse. But of course, he reminded anyway that if anything happened, I was to call him, and he would get to Mom's bedside as soon as possible.

When I got to Mom's room, there was a dramatic difference between how Mom appeared this particular Wednesday morning and the way she had appeared the morning before when I thought she would not make it through the day. It also appeared to me that the medication issue had been resolved. When I asked Mom how she felt that morning, she said that she was feeling no pain. The day was fairly easy going and uneventful as far as what transpired throughout the day.

Mom and I spent most of the morning talking about all kinds of little things. We talked about anything that came to mind with the exception of talking about the elephant that was in the room, that being about her present condition.

To me, it just seemed like we were trying to catch up on all the happenings and things that we had not talked about before and for so many years. It seemed that we both were trying in a matter of a few minutes or hours to make up for all those lost years. Of course, throughout the day, we were oftentimes interrupted by the nursing staff. I really could not complain about those interruptions as the nursing staff was very diligent in their desire to make sure Mom was in no pain and that all her vital signs and so forth were where they should be.

All in all, that Wednesday ended up being a very quiet and uneventful day. Mom and I just continued to talk and try to catch up on years of relationship gone by. Other than the times I left Mom's room so the nurses could attend to Mom's needs, we spent the entire day together. As I was getting ready to leave for the day, Mom asked me when my sister was coming. I told her that Sarah would be in Rochester on the coming Friday night. I also told her that I would be picking her up at the airport and bringing her right to the hospital to see her. Mom smiled and shook her head and said, somewhat ominously, "Well, I can wait that long I guess." It almost seemed like Mom knew something that she was not letting anyone else know about. I left Mom's room, telling her again that I would see her in the morning.

Thursday morning started out just like all the other mornings had since Mom had been in the hospital. By the time I got there that morning, Mom had already ordered her coffee and two pieces of bacon. The nurses were coming in and out of the room to see if Mom was in any pain and if she needed anything at all.

Once again, I was really impressed with the care that was being provided to my mom by all the nursing staff. If she needed anything at all, she only needed to call them, and they were always right there meeting her every need. The nurses were constantly checking on her pain level and if she needed any medication to control her pain. They were constantly adjusting her position in the bed in their effort to keep her as comfortable as possible. Under all the circumstances, I believe the nursing staff provided Mom with the best care possible and that anyone could reasonably expect.

Rob stayed in Austin that Thursday morning to work, and Sarah would not arrive until the next day. This gave mom and I the ability to spend yet another entire day talking some more and to discuss all the things that needed to be done in order for her to come home. We talked quite a bit about making the arrangements necessary for her when she was finally able to leave the hospital and return home.

Of course, Mom being the forever penny-pincher, she was, as always, concerned about the cost of her in-home care. We talked about how much she would have to spend on in-home care. We also talked about the alternatives of going home versus being in a hospice or a nursing home. Let us say that the subject of going into a nursing home was less than well-received and was not discussed anymore after that one conversation. However, Mom did concede the possibility of such a course of action and suggested to me that "maybe you should check into how much it would cost to go into a care facility if I can't go home." I said that I would do that and left the topic alone after that.

The rest of the day passed quietly with little interruption other than the nurses again coming and going about their care for Mom. As with each day, it eventually came time for me to go home. As I was getting ready to leave, Mom said she just wanted me to know one thing. I asked her "What is that?" She said that she loved me and was glad I was there with her. I told her that I loved her and even gave her a kiss on her forehead.

Two amazing things had just happened. That was the first time I had told my mother I loved her in so many years I could not remember. It was also the first time I had kissed my mom in nearly thirty years. It was hard for me then, as well as now, to imagine how my actions over the years had done to undermine and destroy the relationship between my mother and me. At a time like my mom was facing then, my relationship between my mom and I should have been much healthier than it was and was only "on the rocks" as a result of my actions over the years. Now, in a matter of a few days, we seemed to be trying to restore our relationship to what it should have been.

Mom then made a comment that struck me as a little strange. As I was leaving, she said, "You know, I just have a feeling that there is still something I need to learn." I found this to be an interesting comment given all my mom's years of teaching and studying to now still feeling like she needed to learn something new. I asked her if she had any idea of what she meant by thinking she needed to learn something. "No, I just have this really strong feeling that there is something I need to learn," was all she said.

"Well, if you figure out what it is that you need to learn, let me know," was the last thing I said to her as I finally headed out the door. "I will see you in the morning, Mom," I said as I left.

As I drove home, I could not get Mom's statement of her need to learn something out of my mind. What could she possibly mean by saying that she felt she still needed to learn "something?" How could she and what could she learn about "something" in the hospital? Maybe it meant that she really believed she could be going home and needed to learn what her limitations at home might be.

I did not know what to make of her statement. All I know is that night, just before going to bed I prayed one simple little prayer. I prayed to God, "Please let her have enough time to learn whatever it is she feels she needs to learn." I would soon learn that God does answer prayers and that sometimes they are answered in magnificent and wondrous ways.

Chapter Eighteen

Friday morning and, in fact, all day Friday became a whole day that I will never forget as long as I live. After I had prayed the night before asking God to give Mom enough time to "learn" what it was she needed to learn, I had given no more thought to Mom's statement that she had made the day before when she said that she "needed to learn something."

I was in for such a shock that Friday morning that if I had given any thought about Mom's "need to learn something," I may have been better prepared for what transpired over the course of the entire day. First, I never expected the greeting that I got or what I would learn myself and witness that day.

I was quite surprised when I got to Mom's room. She was propped up in bed with a cup of coffee in front of her with a strange and unusual smile on her face. In the pit of my stomach, I seemed to sense some "aura" around her and the hairs on my arm stood up. "How are you today?" I asked not really sure of what to expect for an answer. Mom said, "I am fine, but I have something that is really important that I need to tell you."

"Okay," I said; and instead of just sitting down in the chair that was across the room and next to the wall like I usually did, I pulled that chair right up next to her bedside and sat down. I had never pulled the chair up to the bed before, and it really didn't dawn on me that I had done so. I really couldn't explain the feeling I was having, but I felt like I was in a different room than I had been in all week. "So what's so important?" I asked.

My mom grabbed my hand with more force than I could ever remember her grabbing me and was physically pulling me even closer to her. She was pulling me with such force that I almost felt like I was going to fall out of the chair. "I had a dream last night," she informed me with such emotion that I knew I had better pay attention.

"Really, what about?" seemed to be a very logical question for me to ask. With that brilliant question, Mom began to tell me about her dream.

She started to relay her dream to me. "I started out by finding myself sitting in a wheelchair. I was being pushed by someone down this very long hallway. It was very comfortable in the hallway, and I didn't feel out of place or uncomfortable at all. And I did not feel afraid. In fact, I was feeling very comfortable and was enjoying myself. I could feel the warmth all around me while I was in that hallway. The hallway was well lit. I had no idea where I was going. But the further I went, the better I felt. I could not see where the light was coming from, but it was all around me. I could not see any source of heat either. The hallway was just so completely comfortable and inviting," she said.

"I could see pictures hanging on both sides of the hallway. The pictures were of your dad, his parents, my parents and friends of mine that had died several years ago." I suddenly sat forward in my chair and started to pay very close attention to what she was saying.

"What happened then?" I asked.

"When we got to the end of the hallway, there was a wooden wall. The wooden wall blocked the entire end of the hallway. There was no door or windows, and I did not see any way of getting through the wall. When we got right to the end of the hallway and right up against the wooden wall, whoever was pushing me in the wheel chair actually just seemed to push me right through the wooden wall." I felt like I was glued to my chair sitting on the edge so as to not miss any of what Mom was telling me about her dream.

Mom continued, "As I was pushed and went through the wooden wall, I was not scratched, cut, or hurt in anyway. In fact, I didn't feel anything at all. Suddenly, when I was through the wall, I was instantly in a very beautiful garden.

"The garden was more beautiful than anything I have ever seen. There were trees, beautiful flowers everywhere, and pretty green grass. The sky was a beautiful blue with very white and puffy clouds in it. There were little children playing everywhere in the garden, and I could hear them laughing and watch them as they played. "It was obvious that they were very happy and having a good time playing. It was so beautiful, and I really enjoyed it there. I did not want to ever leave."

"What happened after that?" I asked her, anxiously waiting for her response. Sounding very dejected and disappointed, Mom said, "I woke up in this bed."

"Well, that was quite a dream," I responded as I sat back in my chair.

"Wait, that wasn't the end of it," Mom said.

"Okay, so what happened then?" I asked again, not entirely sure where this dream was heading.

"Well, after a short time, I fell back to sleep and began to dream again. This time, I was not being pushed down a warm, well-lighted, and inviting hallway. I was actually being chased. I was screaming and running as fast as I could. I was trying as hard as I could to get away from whoever it was that was chasing me. The hallway was black, dark, frightening, and I could smell something burning. There was no warm air surrounding me. There were no pictures on the wall, only what appeared to be flashing lightning bolts and thunder, and it seemed like the wind was blowing. There was no light other than the lightning. It was so cold, uncomfortable, and frightening. I don't ever remember being so scared in all my life. The entire time I was being chased, the lightning bolts kept flashing on the walls, and I never saw anyone. But I could hear someone chasing me the whole time. I felt completely alone. I was running and screaming as I was chased by someone or something."

I was now literally back on the edge of my chair. I had a belief that I knew what I was hearing and what the underlying story of this dream was. I could hardly wait to hear the end of this dream. Mom's grip on my arm became much stronger as she continued with describing this dream she had had. There was absolutely no sound in her room that I heard while I waited for her to continue. It even seemed hard for me to get my breath as I waited.

"When I got to the end of the hallway, there was a solid concrete wall with no door and no windows. It was a dead end, and there was no place for me to go. Whoever or whatever was chasing me was getting closer and closer, and I continued to scream as loud as I could. I have never been so frightened in all my life," she said again.

"What did you do then?" I quietly asked.

"I turned to my right, and suddenly there was a door there. I opened the door, and there was a glass window."

"What happened then?" I continued to ask.

"I jumped through the glass window," was Mom's response.

"Where did you go after jumping through the window?" seemed like a logical question.

Again, sounding somewhat disheartened, she said, "I woke up in this bed again."

"Well, what do you think it means?" I asked, knowing full well what I thought it meant.

"That wasn't the end of it," Mom replied and continued with her story without me asking her what happened next.

"Well, I fell back to sleep, and I started dreaming again. When I went back to sleep, both of the hallways were in my vision. The hallways altered and flashed back and forth between the warm, well-lit hallway with the pictures of my family and friends on the wall and the dark, cold, frightening hallway with lightning flashes and someone chasing me and me running and screaming. This back and forth flashing between the two hallways happened many times. It was while this flashing back and forth was going on that I felt someone put their arm around me and asked me, 'Well, Ann, which do you choose?'"

I don't think I had taken a breath during the whole time she was telling me this part of her dream. "Well, which did you choose?" I managed to whisper.

"I chose the lighted hallway, the warm hallway, the hallway with pictures in it," she replied as if she could not believe I had to ask her. "I wanted to be in the field with the trees, the flowers, the green grass, and the little children playing."

I had to find out if Mom knew what had happened to her or what is was that she had experienced. I asked her, "Do you know who it was that put their arm around you?"

"Yes, I do. It was him," she almost shouted out as her finger pointed to the opposite wall of her hospital room. I turned to look and found myself staring into a picture of the face of Jesus Christ that was hanging on the opposite wall. I almost broke down crying right then and there.

"Do you know what your choice means?" I asked.

"Yes, I do," was mom's answer. "I have always believed in Jesus Christ, but I have never really acknowledged him or said it."

"Yes," I said.

"But what does your choice mean?"

"It means that I choose Jesus Christ," she said through her tears.

"You really have chosen Jesus Christ," I announced excitedly to both her and me, as if my pronouncement added anything to the glorious salvation that I was witnessing that morning.

We were both crying and holding on to each other. "I now know what you meant when you asked your dad about his relationship with Jesus Christ," she said through her continuing tears. In that exact moment, all the guilt and negative feelings that I had felt because of the outburst in my dad's hospital room those so many years ago was gone. These were tears of joy that we were both shedding. Then I asked my mom a question that I really never thought or believed I would ever be saying to my mom. "Can we pray?" I asked.

"Yes, I would like that" she said.

So right there, her in her hospital bed and me sitting right beside her, holding each other's hands, we prayed the prayer of salvation as my mom accepted Jesus Christ as her Lord and Savior. The wonderfulness of that prayer was not the end of an incredible day.

After we had dried our tears, we talked about how Mom felt. "I feel like a huge burden had been lifted off of me," she offered. She could not stop smiling. Her whole demeanor was changed. The "aura" that I had seen when I first came into her room remained on her and around her all day. For the rest of the day, if you did not want to hear about Mom's salvation dream, you had better not come into her room.

In Mark 16:15, Jesus tells us to "go ye into all the nations and preach the gospel to every creature." Mom was not able to do that because of her confinement to her hospital bed. However, everyone, and I mean everyone, who came into Mom's room on that Friday was told the story of her dream and her salvation and how Jesus Christ had saved her.

It did not matter if you were a nurse, a nurse's aide, the woman who delivered her meals, the resident who was her doctor, the attending physician and all the residents, interns, and medical students with him. Everyone was told of how Jesus Christ had saved her. Even my nieces were told Mom's salvation story when they came to see their grandma later that day.

My mom told the word of salvation, through her newfound faith and belief in Jesus Christ, to anyone and everyone who came in the door. There was not a single person who, when Mom began to tell her story, made an excuse to leave the room. No one failed to take the time to listen to a new salvation story.

Not only did she relay her story of salvation to everyone who came into her room, but many of those she told were in tears as they left the room. This tearful group included both her oncologist and her attending physician. I believe more seeds were planted for the Lord that morning than I had ever seen. Shamefully, there were more seeds planted by my mom on that day than I have planted in so many years. I felt, and still feel, truly blessed to have been involved in such a moving and wonderful experience. But as I later would learn, the moving and wonderful experience was far from over.

The rest of the day, that Friday passed fairly quickly and quietly after Mom had relayed her salvation story to all who came into her room. Mom and I spent the time talking about her newly found life in Jesus Christ. Mom seemed so happy. She did manage to surprise me yet again a little later on that day.

While we were talking later that day, suddenly, at one point, she said to me, "I am sorry."

"Sorry about what?" I asked.

"I am sorry that the church let you kids down," was her stunning comment. The first thought that came to my mind was Mom telling me, during my dad's final days that she was sure my dad would go to heaven because he "went to church every Sunday." It was as if now my mom realized that going to church does not save you, that being a good person does not save you, and that doing good deeds does not save you. Mom now knew that only with a personal relationship with Jesus Christ as your Lord and Savior are you truly saved.

Mom and I continued to talk for a while about the difference between attending church and having a personal relationship with Jesus Christ. I told Mom that she should not worry about what the church may or may not have done. I told her that the really important thing was that she had made an awesome decision and could now just enjoy her new relationship with the Lord. I also mentioned, maybe to ease her mind a little, that I believe the fact that Dad's picture was in the hallway that she had chosen was a sign that Dad had established a relationship with Jesus and that he was with Jesus now.

Before I knew it, the time had come for me to go and pick up Sarah at the airport. I told Mom that I was going to get Sarah and that I would bring her right back to the hospital. I left Mom's room and the hospital to pick up my sister at the airport.

Chapter Nineteen

As I drove to the airport, Mom's comment about her church kept going through my mind. I was not sure how Sarah might receive Mom's "dream" as Sarah had never really been open to any discussion of religion or faith. I wondered how Sarah would take our Mom's salvation story. Part of me was even a little concerned at that scene that may be created. Wouldn't you think that, at some point, I would learn to trust the Lord as he is about his own business?

When I arrived at the airport, Sarah's plane was just landing, so the timing was perfect. I met Sarah at the gate where we said our hellos and exchanged a big hug. I headed to the baggage carousel when Sarah told me, "I don't have any baggage. I carried on everything."

"How long are you going to be able to stay?" I asked.

"Well, I have ten days if I need them, but I would like to get back to my students as soon as possible," was her response. We loaded her carry-on into the car and headed to the hospital.

"How is Mom doing?" was the first question Sarah asked as we headed from the airport to the highway leading to the hospital. Not wanting to let on to anything that had transpired that morning, my somewhat cryptic response was "today, she is doing really great."

"Really?" was Sarah's quizzical response.

"Yep, but I will let her tell you all about it," was another one of my brilliant replies.

"I am glad I got here when I did," Sarah offered.

"Well, I know Mom will be glad to see you,"

I said. Suddenly, Sarah started crying and blurted out, "I can't believe this is happening."

"I know, but I know Mom really wants to talk to you," I replied. After that brief exchange, we pretty much drove in silence the remaining short distance to the hospital. Given all that had happened up to that point, I was not sure of what to expect when Mom and Sarah got together. I guessed only time would tell.

I parked the car, and Sarah almost jumped out of the car while it was still moving. We quickly crossed the street from the parking garage and made our way to the elevators and up to Mom's room. When we walked in the door of Mom's room, Sarah hurried across the floor with tears in her eyes to say hello to Mom and to give her a big hug. As Sarah started talking, Mom said, "I have something really important I have to tell you," which stopped Sarah instantly.

"What is it?" Sarah wanted to know. *Here it comes*, I thought to myself as I sat in the chair across the room from Mom and Sarah.

I have no doubt that mom knew that Sarah had made several comments about her "lack" of faith and that religion of any sort was not a serious matter to her. I knew this because Mom and I had talked about it that Thursday before Mom went into the hospital. Now, as Sarah sat at Mom's bedside, Mom took Sarah's arm and began to retell the "dreams" Mom had the night before. She left out no details, and Mom's voice was filled with a great deal of emotion.

Mom was retelling her story to Sarah as if Sarah was the only person in the world that she had to tell her story to. I watched as my sister became very still and somewhat pale as the Good News was told to her for perhaps the first time. Watching the workings of God, as Mom related her salvation story, on my sister was remarkable. When Mom finished, Sarah was in tears, and Mom turned to me and smiled. It was a smile that seemed to say, "There, I told her, and now the choice is up to her." But, as it turned out, this was not the only message my sister would receive.

I said nothing to either my mom or my sister. Instead, I just sat there and watched the interaction between Mom and Sarah. There were several minutes of silence, and I noticed Mom was looking at Sarah with a completely new look in her eye. I got the distinct feeling, and it was my belief, that Mom felt that she had accomplished a very important part of her witness by sharing the story of her salvation dreams with Sarah. Little did I know at that time that I would hear an even more supernatural intercession in the life of my mom and sister before the afternoon was finished.

Mom and Sarah talked for a while longer about what one would suspect would be the type of issues that you may have with your mother. Sarah told Mom a lot of what was going on in her life. This included the fact that Sarah's husband, Wolfgang, deeply regretted the fact that he was not able to come for a visit. As Sarah explained, Wolfgang's sister was also very ill, suffering from cancer herself and that he needed to stay home with and for her.

The conversation grew less and less; and after a bit, Mom said, "I am kind of tired and would like to take a nap now." Sarah and I both said okay, and together we headed out of Mom's room to go to the cafeteria to get something to eat so that Mom could take her nap.

Once Sarah and I got to the cafeteria, we got ourselves something to eat and sat down at one of the tables. While we were sitting there, Sarah asked me how I felt and what I felt about Mom's dream. Stepping way outside of my comfort zone, I told Sarah that I was very grateful that Mom had had her dream and that she had been able to make her own decision regarding Jesus. I also told her that I was very happy that her decision would lead her to heaven with her newfound Savior.

Personally, I felt that was a pretty gutsy statement for me to make to Sarah given the contentious history she and I had over the years about the issue of salvation. Somewhat surprisingly, Sarah made a comment that stuck with me. Sarah's comment was "well, my beliefs are my beliefs." There was not much I could say to that comment, but I have often wondered exactly what her "beliefs" were and what they meant to her. We finished our cafeteria meal and headed back upstairs to Mom's room.

Sarah and I spent the remainder of that afternoon continuing the meaningless prattle of people who do not know what to say to each other under circumstances like those facing us then. Sarah sat next to Mom and held her hand the whole time we were there. She kept asking Mom if she was in pain, and Mom would answer that she was fine. Sarah asked this question so much that, at one point, she finally told Sarah, "I will let you know when I am in pain." She did too. If she began to feel any pain, she would tell us to get the nurse, which we did, and the nurse would quickly arrive with Mom's pain medication.

CHAPTER TWENTY

When it came time to leave for the day, I was to be yet again amazed at how the Lord was working in Mom's life and the life of my sister. I went to Mom's bed, leaned over, and gave her a kiss, telling her again that I loved her and that I would be back to see her in the morning. While I was still standing at the side of Mom's bed, Sarah came over, leaned over, and gave Mom a kiss.

It was at that exact moment that I believe the Holy Spirit manifested himself in that hospital room. As Sarah leaned over to give Mom a goodbye kiss, Mom grabbed Sarah's wrist with noticeable force. I could tell, by the look on Sarah's face, that Mom had indeed grabbed her with some considerable force. Mom pulled Sarah very close to her, and it was then that a voice came from my mom's mouth that was neither my mom's voice nor was it any voice I had ever heard before; and with words that could not have come from my mom's knowledge or understanding, Mom "spoke" to my sister.

The room was incredibly still and quiet. There was no sound that I could hear, none of the usual hustle-and-bustle sounds associated with a hospital surrounding. The steady noise from the nurse's station just outside my mom's room was gone. There was no sound at all other than the voice coming out of my mom's mouth. The voice coming from Mom was strong and resolute in its tenor. It was not the voice of a frail and dying woman. Then, in this unknown voice and in unequivocal terms, strongly and firmly said to my sister, "Your denial of me is false. Your denial of me is false." (Psalm 119:118) That was all that was said. Mom let go of Sarah's wrist, turned her head away from Sarah, and almost instantly she fell asleep.

Sarah was quite visibly shaken and stunned. She stood at Mom's bedside for a few moments without saying anything. After a little bit,

Sarah looked at me with kind of a questioning look. She was crying and never said anything to me until we got to the car where she again said, although in a whisper now, "My beliefs are my beliefs." I knew, in my heart and mind and without a doubt, that the Holy Spirit had spoken to my sister and that a huge and precious seed had been planted. We drove home without further comment from either of us regarding what had occurred at Mom's beside.

When we got home, Sarah said that she was tired and was going to bed. With nothing else said between us other than good night, we both turned in for the night. I prayed that night that Sarah would hear the message she had been given and change her beliefs and ultimately come to know Jesus Christ as her Savior. Regardless if she did that night or not, I was certain that she had been exposed to something she had never experienced before. But then again, so had I.

Saturday morning was a bright, sunny day as both Sarah and I headed to back to the hospital. It was a quiet ride for me as Sarah decided to ride to the hospital with Rob. I believed that Sarah was still somewhat stunned by the experience she had and what had been told to her the day before.

Rob, Sarah, and I all met at the hospital. It was the same routine as usual as we all got to the hospital at about 10:00 o'clock that morning. We headed up the elevator; and when we got the fourth floor, we went right into Mom's room. Yet again and one more time, I was not prepared for what I was to witness that day.

Just as we were entering Mom's room, the nurse was just leaving the room, and the attending physician was in the room talking with Mom. As we entered the room, the doctor indicated that he would like to talk to the three of us. We told Mom that we would be right back and left to go to what turned out to be the "death conference." I knew, in my gut, what was coming.

The doctor took us to a small room and informed us that there was really nothing more they could do for Mom other than to keep her comfortable for however much time she had left. He told us the tumors were very fast growing and that she just did not have the strength to fight much longer. He told us that Mom could die from the cancer, or she could die from a pneumonia she had now contracted. There were just no more options.

The doctor asked us if we knew what Mom wanted to do in a situation like this. Through his suddenly appearing tears, Rob offered that Mom had made a living will and that she had made her wishes very clear. He also told us that Mom had created a medical power of attorney, giving Rob the power to make medical decisions if Mom was unable to do so.

After several more questions from the doctor to us and us to the doctor, it was decided that as long as Mom was able to make the decisions for herself, then she should be the one to make those decisions. I did ask the doctor if he thought Mom was competent enough to make those decisions given the pain medication she was on and so forth. He indicated to us that he felt Mom was fully competent to make those decisions that needed to be made.

The doctor got up to leave and told us to stay in the room as long as we wanted. He told us that he was going to talk with Mom and see what she wanted to do. We all sat there in a numb silence as we each contemplated what we had just been told. Hadn't it only been a couple of days ago that we were told the plan was to get Mom home, and now we have been told that there is nothing more that can be done? It just didn't seem right. Our mom was dying, and there was not a darn thing that we could do about it. Both Sarah and Rob were wracked with sobs and tears. I do not believe I had ever seen my brother crying so hard. They were not alone.

I felt the deep impending sense of loss, but I think I also felt reassured now that Mom had made an eternal decision that would ultimately and finally relieve her of all her pain and suffering and that would take her to a better place when the end did come. I selfishly hoped it would be a little while in coming, but I think I was more prepared and ready for the end than either Sarah or Rob. After a few more minutes in the room, the three of us headed down the hallway back to Mom's room.

When we entered Mom's, she was all by herself. She was not upset or crying. She was just sitting there with a small smile on her face. "I told them I did not want them doing anything other than keeping me out of pain," she offered without prompting from any of us. "This is my decision and that is what I have decided," she continued. "I don't want you three to be upset about this, but I do not want to suffer the pain associated with the treatment that was suggested. I do not want anymore surgeries or anything like that. Just keep my pain under control," was her directive to all of us. We three kids looked at each other and agreed. "If that is your decision, then that is your decision," we kind of all said together.

"It is," she said, and that was all she said about it. Her decision was never a topic of conversation again.

We spent a few more hours with Mom that day. We talked about all sorts of petty things that in the totality of the situation seemed meaningless. I guess that is what some, if not most, people do when faced with the impending death of someone they love. Even so, it was hard for us to stay there. In fact, Rob was struggling mightily to keep from crying in front of Mom. He gave up the fight to keep from crying by blurting out, "I have things I have to do."

Mom, Sarah, and I all said, "Okay, but be careful," as we knew he was going out to ride his Harley Davidson motorcycle to try and clear his head, and I guess to temporarily forget about what was happening. Again, it was Sarah and I that spent a few more minutes with Mom before saying we were going to go downstairs to the cafeteria again to get something to eat. "Okay, see you when you get back," Mom said. Those were the last words Mom ever spoke directly to either of us.

After Sarah and I finished in the cafeteria, we went back up to Mom's room. In the short period of time we had been gone, a drastic and dramatic change had occurred since we left. Mom was asleep, and we had a great deal of difficulty in waking her up. When we finally got her awake, she was just lying in bed, staring at the ceiling, and she never said a word to either of us. This was really quite unnerving under the circumstances. Mom continued to lie in bed, staring at the ceiling and never saying a word to us for the rest of the morning and into the early afternoon.

Mom's pastor came by later that Saturday afternoon to see how Mom was doing. Mom remained in the bed, still and continuing to stare fixedly at the ceiling. "Ann," the pastor said. "It is Pastor Elizabeth. Can you hear me?" she asked as she leaned over the bed. Mom blinked and turned slowly to look at the pastor and nodded a small affirmative nod. "Are you okay?" was the next question from the pastor. Again, Mom made a small affirmative nod and then returned to staring at the ceiling.

"What are you looking at?" was the next question from Pastor Elizabeth. It was Mom's response to that question that I was again amazed at what I was witnessing while wondering what was going through my sister's mind when she heard Mom's response. I even wondered what was going through the pastor's mind in hearing Mom's answer.

My mom again turned slowly toward the pastor and, in a quiet but very clear voice, said, "I am looking at Jesus." Silence! There was complete, absolute, and deafening silence. There was a total and complete quiet unlike anything I had ever witnessed except the day before when I believe the Holy Spirit spoke through my mother.

After what seemed like several minutes, the pastor asked Mom, "Is he talking to you?"

"Yes," was Mom's only response.

Pastor Elizabeth continued, "What is he saying to you?"

One more slow turn from Mom who replied, "He is telling me to come be with Him." Complete and utter silence again filled the room. You really could have heard a pin drop. What does, or can, one say when in the presence of the Lord?

After a few more moments of this stunned silence, Pastor Elizabeth stood up and looked at Sarah for a few seconds and then said, "Well, I have other people to see today, so I think I will be going." We wished her well, thanked her for coming to see Mom, and we told her to have a good day. Personally, I was left wondering if Pastor Elizabeth had ever experienced the presence of the Lord in that manner and if she was even sure how to deal with it.

Mom had returned to staring at the ceiling; and as Sarah and I watched Mom went to sleep, I never saw my mom awake after that. I never heard my mom speak another word after her letting us know that Jesus was calling her. We left Mom's room shortly thereafter and headed home. I believe that my mom listened to Jesus and his invitation; and shortly after she fell asleep, her soul accepted the invitation to be with her newfound Lord.

It was not until the next morning, shortly after Sarah and I arrived at the hospital that Sunday morning, that Mom's physical body caught up with her. Mom died very peacefully Sunday morning. I gave her a goodbye kiss. Now she lives forever with her Lord; and my consolation is that I know that, through the grace of God, I will see her again in the future.

My mom's funeral was held on the following Tuesday after her death. We did this so Sarah could be there before having to go back to Germany. We did not have a traditional funeral service as it was Mom's wish to be cremated and buried with my dad. My mom and dad had been married for thirty-one years; and now, I believe, with Mom's dream identifying my dad's picture on the wall in the hallway in her dream that lead her to salvation, that they are together again.

We did hold a memorial service for Mom. Some seventy or so of her friends, work acquaintances, neighbors, and others attended. The service was held in the church that Mom attended, where we kids had been baptized and confirmed in and that Sarah had been married in. Mom's pastor, Pastor Elizabeth, spoke a few words in accordance with the traditions of her church. I was given the opportunity to say something at the service. There was no doubt in my mind about what I was going to say.

As it came time for me to speak, I stood up in front of those in attendance and related the story of Mom's dream, what it meant, and how it led to her salvation. I am not sure of how all the people took this message. I do know, from looking at the faces of those people before me, that many of them were in tears as I related Mom's salvation story. I looked at my brother and sister, seated in the front row, and witnessed both of them again in wracking sobs with tears rolling down their faces.

I cannot say what, if any, deep or meaningful impact Mom's dream and my retelling it had on my brother and sister. Neither can I tell what impact, if any, it had on those in attendance at Mom's memorial service. No more that I can tell what, if any, impact Mom's dream will have on those who read the recounting of it in this short book.

All I know for sure is that the love of God, through His Son, Jesus Christ, gave my mother the time she needed to "learn" that "God so loved the world, that he gave His only begotten Son, that whosoever believeth in Him should not perish, but have everlasting life" (John 3:16).

We have all been given this same chance. We have all been given this same love. We must all decide for ourselves if we want to choose Jesus or choose the alternative of eternal separation from God. There are no other choices, "There is no other name under heaven given among men, whereby we must be saved" (Acts 4:14).

We must all look to ourselves in this decision-making responsibility. We have only two choices. Either choice provides for an eternity somewhere. Will you choose to spend eternity with and in the presence of the living God, who is love, or will you decide to spend eternity separated from God forever and to be "cast... into a furnace of fire [where] there shall be wailing and gnashing of teeth" (Matthew 13:42)?

Again, I thank God that my mother was given the time to make this decision for herself even as she lay dying in the hospital. However, we cannot trust that we each will have this same opportunity at the last minute to make this decision. The choice is yours. May the grace of God help you in this decision if you have not already entered into the family of God, and may you come to know the Lord Jesus Christ as your personal Savior.

There is no time to waste. We cannot guarantee the next breath or the next heartbeat. Decide which way you want to go, which hallway you want to choose if you will. I earnestly pray that you make the right choice.

Then if you have prayed that the Lord Jesus Christ come into your life as your personal Lord and Savior and you have asked Him to forgive you your sins, find a church that teaches of the goodness of Jesus and the eternal salvation that is in Him, that is only through Him, and spend time there and with other believers.

May God bless each and every one of you.

ABOUT THE AUTHOR

A baby boomer, born eight short years after the end of World War II, Brent was raised by his mother and father in Southern Minnesota some one hundred miles south of Minneapolis. During his youth, Brent attended elementary school, junior high, and senior high school in Austin, Minnesota. Upon his graduation from high school, Brent attended Austin Junior College, where he was awarded his associate degree in June of 1973.

After graduating from Austin Junior College, Brent enrolled at Winona State University in Winona, Minnesota. The year after enrolling, Brent left Winona State University and enlisted in the United States Air Force in 1974. Brent served in the Air Force at Ellsworth Air Force Base, South Dakota, from 1974 until his honorable discharge in 1978.

Following his discharge from the Air Force, Brent went to work in the fine men's wear clothing business in Rapid City, South Dakota. Brent worked in the clothing business for two years before accepting a position in the food and beverage department of the historic Hotel Alex Johnson in Rapid City. Shortly thereafter, Brent was given the opportunity to become general manager of the Days Inn motel in Rapid City. It was as a result of that employment that Brent was recruited to a manager position in the Green Street Social Club in Salt Lake, Utah. After a year in Salt Lake City, Brent decided to return to school to finish his undergraduate degree and then attempt to enter law school.

Returning to South Dakota, Brent enrolled in Black Hills State University where he graduated Magna Cum Laude with a bachelor of science degree in business administration in 1989. Upon his graduation, Brent was accepted into Thomas M. Cooley law school in Lansing, Michigan. In January 1993, Brent was awarded his Juris Doctorate. Brent practiced law in Lansing, Michigan, for almost eight years, leaving the practice of law in 2001 and returning to the food and beverage business.

Brent has been married to his lovely wife, Theresa, for sixteen years.

CPSIA information can be obtained
at www.ICGtesting.com
Printed in the USA
LVHW031452261120
672639LV00004B/365